2003

University of St. Francis Library

P9-AQM-324

Creating Collaborative and Inclusive Schools

2003

Creating Collaborative
and Inclusive Schools

◆ ◆ ◆ ◆ ◆ ◆ ◆ ◆ ◆ ◆ ◆ ◆ ◆

Lorna Idol

pro·ed
An International Publisher

8700 Shoal Creek Boulevard
Austin, Texas 78757-6897
800/897-3202   Fax 800/397-7633
www.proedinc.com

LIBRARY
UNIVERSITY OF ST. FRANCIS
JOLIET, ILLINOIS

© 2002 by PRO-ED, Inc.
© 1997 by Lorna Idol
8700 Shoal Creek Boulevard
Austin, Texas 78757-6897
800/897-3202   Fax 800/397-7633
www.proedinc.com

All rights reserved. No part of the material protected by this copyright notice may be reproduced or used in any form or by any means, electronic or mechanical, including photocopying, recording, or by any information storage and retrieval system, without prior written permission of the copyright owner.

NOTICE: PRO-ED grants permission to the user of this book to make copies of all appendixes except Appendixes 2.A and 4.A for educational or clinical purposes. Duplication of this material for commercial use is prohibited.

Library of Congress Cataloging-in-Publication Data

Idol, Lorna.
    Creating collaborative and inclusive schools / Lorna Idol—1st ed.
      p.   cm
    Includes bibliographical references and index.
    ISBN 0-89079-877-X (alk. paper)
    1. Inclusive education.   2. Inclusive education—Case studies.
    3. School management and organization.   4. School management and organization—Case studies.   5. Classroom management.
    6. Classroom management—Case studies.   7. Teaching teams.
    8. Teaching teams—Case studies. I. Title.

LC1200 .I36 2002
371.2—dc21   2001019788

This book is designed in Goudy and Frutiger.

Printed in the United States of America
1 2 3 4 5 6 7 8 9 10   05 04 03 02 01

371.2
I21

CONTENTS

PREFACE

Collaborative and inclusive schools are created by the adults who work within them. Both inclusion and collaboration are necessary to make education programs available for ALL students. Putnam, Spiegel, and Bruininks (1995) predicted that, in the new millennium, movement toward increased inclusion will occur; the belief that people with disabilities have a right to participate in inclusive environments will prevail; and students with mild disabilities will be educated in general classrooms.

Envision that in collaborative and inclusive schools all students with special learning and behavioral needs are educated on the same campus as other students attending their neighborhood school. Envision that all staff members share the belief that all educators in the school are ultimately responsible for all students. Envision that the staff members expect that all students will be included with same-age peers for either educational or socialization purposes to the maximum extent possible, with a decision-making team reaching consensus on the type of inclusion that is appropriate in each individual case. Envision that appropriate modifications and adjustments will be made for those students with special learning and behavioral challenges.

In my experience I have found the best configuration for offering inclusive school programs is the use of collaborative teams of professionals and parents working together to create programs that all involved can support. The collaborative team makes decisions for individual students, who are either special education students to be educated in general education classes or students who are at risk for school failure (see also related works by Thousand & Villa [1990] and Nevin, Thousand, Paolucci-Whitcomb, & Villa [1990]). In each case, the intention of the team is to determine the most educationally enhancing learning environment (see Idol & West, 1993) for the targeted student and to provide the necessary support to achieve that end.

This book is written for practitioners in education, those educators who are ultimately responsible for the development and implementation of collaborative and inclusive schools. Thus, the intended audience is classroom teachers, special education teachers, principals, support staff, and program administrators. This is a practical book with emphasis on how to create collaborative and inclusive schools.

To create a collaborative school is to create a school where the team structure is the primary means by which decisions are made and programs are implemented. In a collaborative school, administrators, faculty, staff, and parents work together in collective and collegial groups. In the collaborative school ALL students are included in the campus-wide educational effort, including those with special education needs. All students are assigned to general classrooms for their educational programs and faculty and staff members teach in various types of team structures to ensure that all students have access to a quality education.

The chapters in this book are organized around a series of questions that have been found important to answer in the development of collaborative and inclusive schools. The answers to the questions are based on my own fieldwork and reflect the results and observations of my consulting and teaching experiences in working with educators in the United States, Canada, Australia, and New Zealand. I wish to express my sincere appreciation to the many educators with whom I have worked. I hope this book is viewed as a celebration of the collective knowledge of many educators who have been challenged to build collaborative and inclusive schools.

In the first chapter, I provide descriptions of three schools where efforts have been made to develop collaborative and inclusive schools. The three schools are from three different levels: elementary, intermediate, and high school. Common themes and individual differences among these schools are explored as a means of setting the stage for the remaining chapters in the book.

Each chapter title is in the form of a question; each question provides the springboard for exploring the various facets of the major areas that need to be addressed in the development and implementation of collaborative and inclusive schools.

CHAPTER ONE

◆◆◆◆◆◆◆◆◆◆◆◆◆◆◆◆◆◆◆◆◆◆◆◆

What Does a Collaborative and Inclusive School Look Like?

◆ In this chapter the two major concepts presented in this book are explored: collaboration and inclusion. Illustrations of how these concepts were implemented in three different levels of schools—elementary, intermediate, and high school—are provided. In each school, the principal and faculty worked together to provide a quality education for all the students attending that school.

The descriptions of these three schools provide the reader with concrete and realistic visions of what a collaborative and inclusive school might look like. Each of these schools is unique; yet, some common themes are woven across the three. In this chapter these themes will be introduced; and then explored in greater detail in the remaining chapters of this book. But in order to understand best what these school descriptions really represent, it is important to first understand what is meant by the words *collaboration* and *inclusion*.

Collaboration

In a collaborative school, administrators, faculty, and the entire school staff anticipate they will be working together in planning, decision making, program implementation, and program evaluation. In the collaborative school, much emphasis is placed on using an effective group decision-making process.

The collaborative effort is an important part of building sound educational programs for all children. The Collaborative Consultation Model, originally developed by Idol, Paolucci-Whitcomb, and Nevin (1986), and more recently revised and refined (Idol, Nevin, & Paolucci-Whitcomb, 1994), has been and can be used to build a collaborative school, an inclusive school where all types of children are educated in the neighborhood school, and a school where there are collaborative programs between general and special education with the express purpose of improving or developing programs for students with special needs and those who are at risk for school failure.

West, Idol, and Cannon (1989) described this purpose as being threefold: (a) to prevent some students from experiencing learning and behavior problems, (b) to remediate certain learning and behavior problems that some students might be experiencing, and (c) to coordinate instructional programs for students who receive instruction through more than one type of program. In the school descriptions that follow, examples can be found for each of these three purposes.

In the original development of the Collaborative Consultation Model for specific use in educating students with special needs in general education programs, collaborative consultation was defined as "an interactive process that enables teams of people with diverse expertise to generate creative solutions to mutually defined problems. The outcome is enhanced and altered from the original solutions that any team member would produce independently" (Idol, Paolucci-Whitcomb, & Nevin, 1986, p. ix). More recently, my co-authors and I (Idol et al., 1994) have expanded application of this model and its collaborative and interactive process to students who are at risk for school failure as well.

Thus, using the definition above, educators could apply the Collaborative Consultation Model in educating any students with learning and behavior challenges in general education programs (see Chapter 2). They could also apply the collaborative, decision-making process (as defined earlier and in more detail in Chapter 3) to improve, enhance, and streamline any problem-solving situation where people are expected to make collective decisions. The collaborative process can be used for effective planning, problem solving, and decision making, thus making it an effective tool for proactive strategic planning.

Educational collaboration is not an end unto itself; it is a catalytic process used in interactive relationships among individuals working toward a mutually defined, concrete vision or outcome (Idol & West, 1991). Educational collaboration as an adult-to-adult, interactive process can be expected to have an indirect impact on student outcomes, with changes in adult teams occurring first. If the attitudes, skills, knowledge, and/or behaviors of the adults involved are changed, you can expect that the impact of these changes on many students will be profound.

Inclusion

In the inclusive school, all students are educated in general education programs. Inclusion is when a student with special learning and/or behavioral needs is educated full time in the general education program. Essentially, *inclusion* means that a student with special education needs is attending the general school program, enrolled in age-appropriate classes 100% of the school day. There are no levels or degrees of inclusion. This is a first and major source of confusion among some educators, and misunderstandings about the difference between mainstreaming and inclusion are common. Many believe that the terms are synonymous. They are not. Mainstreaming is when a student with special education needs is educated partially in a special education program, but to the maximum extent possible educated in the general education program. As stated above, inclusion means a 100% time placement in general education. There is no such thing as partial inclusion, as this is simply a reiteration of what has been done for a long time in the name of mainstreaming (see related discussion in Schloss, 1992).

Sage (1993) has made a clear distinction between mainstreaming and inclusion. First, mainstreaming and similar terms evolved from two parallel school systems (general education and special education) and, second, there is an underlying assumption of inequity between the two systems. This assumption is simply a cultural practice in public education, where special education has become an important but smaller and separate system from that of general education. Thus, in the integration approach, the lesser system members (special education) join the favored majority (mainstream) system. The underlying assumption of mainstreaming is that participation in the majority group will be in accordance with the standards of the dominant system. In contrast, according to Sage, inclusion implies the existence of only one unified educational system that encompasses all members equitably.

Clarification of these two terms often results in people dividing themselves into two different camps: the full inclusion camp and the partial inclusion camp (refer to Fuchs & Fuchs [1994] and Kauffman & Hallahan [1995] for a more in-depth exploration of these and related issues). Actually, the term *full inclusion* is redundant, as inclusion means 100% time in the general education program, and *partial inclusion* is contradictory, as 100% cannot be "partial." Hence, more precise descriptors of these two camps are inclusion for all students versus offering a full continuum of special education services, with inclusion offered as an option for some students.

In the school descriptions that follow, one of the schools was using full inclusion. However, there was a gradual transition period at that school, from initially pulling six students out for supportive instruction to educating all students in the general classes. Included were students with mild learning and behavior problems and students with physical disabilities. In the intermediate school, a radical change was made to include all but six students with severe and multiple handicaps. In the high school, all students were included in some courses, but laboratory courses were also offered for students who needed extra academic support; this option was open to all students, not just to special education students. Students with mild learning and behavior problems were included in this school.

Principal Support

In building collaborative and inclusive schools, the most important element is the support and leadership of the school principal. In a survey of consulting teachers working with classroom teachers (Idol-Maestas & Ritter, 1985), this finding was strongly indicated. Nearly all of the consulting teachers said that support from the principal was the most important factor in whether they were able to successfully support classroom teachers in the inclusive education of special education students.

In my own consulting work with many different school districts and divisions, I have found, regardless of type or amount of staff development, that one factor is crucial. If the teachers to be involved in the development of collaborative and inclusive schools do not have support from the school principal, there is only a very small chance that actual implementation will occur.

In the school descriptions that follow, each of the principals was supportive of the effort and demonstrated strong leadership skills. Each principal was also unique in his or her own way of working with faculty and staff. Supportive of the earlier effective schools' research (Brookover, Beady, Flood, Schweitzer, & Wisenbaker, 1979; Duckett et al., 1980; Edmonds, 1979; Smith & Scott, 1990), principals were viewed by the faculty as instructional leaders, not just as administrative managers. Such principals were actively involved with teachers and were cognizant of instructional and student management needs in the classrooms.

Collaborative and Inclusive Schools

Following are three descriptions of the transitions, growth, and changes that occurred in three different schools where principals and teachers were interested in helping their staff members to be more collaborative and their school to be more inclusive.

Elementary School

In this elementary school, the principal was a former teacher who was a very strong instructional leader. She also had a warm heart and encouraged teachers to be loving and supportive of the students. For example, her office and the front office were filled with teddy bears and complemented by jars of candy. The halls of the school were literally filled with the students' artwork and projects.

The school was a kindergarten through fourth grade school with two classes for each grade level and a morning and afternoon kindergarten class. There was one special education teacher, the youngest teacher in the building, who was accustomed to providing resource instruction in a pull-out situation.

I met the principal and half of the faculty at a staff development institute I was conducting on the topic of building collaborative and inclusive schools. Several important outcomes resulted from our week together. First, the principal scheduled a 2-day retreat, wherein the remainder of the faculty would be educated by those who attended the institute on the key concepts. This second group included the special education teacher, who was somewhat reluctant to engage in inclusion and chose not to attend the first institute.

Second, the principal made a bold decision regarding program finances. She decided to use the federal Chapter 1 monies differently from how they had been used in the past. Formerly, these monies funded one Chapter 1 teacher who offered pull-out resource services. These monies now were combined with special education monies for instructional assistants and some bilingual education monies so that special education students were included. The combined monies allowed the principal to support one full-time instructional assistant for every two classroom teachers, or in other words, one assistant for every grade level and one for the kindergarten program.

The faculty determined that these assistants would be used for instructional purposes, not clerical work, and that they would be under the supervision of the classroom teachers to whom they were assigned. This decision also resulted in the grade level teachers working more closely as a team, as they shared an instructional assistant.

Third, during the retreat, the faculty formulated job descriptions for the role of the special education teacher as a cooperating teacher and for the instructional assistants. These job descriptions can be found in Chapter 5. Fourth, the principal and faculty decided to use a site-based decision-making team as an administrative structure for the building and as an advisory group to the principal.

In the first year of these major changes it was informative and interesting to watch how the attitudes and approaches of the adults involved changed. For example, at the beginning of the year, the special education teacher felt very strongly that six students eligible for specialized instruction for dyslexia should be taught in the resource room. By the end of the first school year, five of these students were totally included and the sixth student was pulled out for only 30 minutes a week. By the beginning of the second year, no students were pulled out. Thus, the special education teacher's attitude changed favorably during the year.

Another very important change was the classroom teachers' attitudes toward the inclusion efforts. Paramount to this was that the faculty, as a group at their retreat, decided to move forward with inclusion.

An additional significant change was in how the classroom teachers used the support and services of the special education teacher. In the beginning, the teachers agreed that the cooperating teacher role, in which the specialist works in the classroom with students with special needs, was the way they would all use the special education teacher's services. Yet, as the year progressed and they became more proficient in using the instructional assistants, there was a split in how the special education services were used. About half the teachers preferred to use the cooperating teacher model and about half preferred the consulting teacher role for the special education teacher. Consulting teachers confer with classroom teachers, particularly as methods and materials specialists, but do not work directly with students (see Chapter 5 for a more detailed discussion of these two support staff roles). The special education teacher was very willing to accommodate the requests of the classroom teacher and moved back and forth comfortably between the two roles.

It took some time for the classroom teachers to get used to having instructional assistants. Even though they had prepared a job description for the assistants, the teachers still had to experiment and make adjustments in order to grow accustomed to having someone else in their classrooms. They had to work more closely with other teachers teaching at the same grade level and maximize the support available to them through the special education teacher.

The last change is very revealing as it pertains to changes in attitudes toward students with disabling conditions. At the beginning of the first year of inclusion, the teachers unanimously agreed that it would be more difficult to include students with physical disabilities. As they developed an outstanding program for a girl in the third grade with severe cerebral palsy, their attitudes changed. By midyear they felt the most difficult-to-include students were those with learning disabilities, especially if they were in the dyslexia program. Then, as the teachers grew more accustomed to working with the support staff, making instructional and curricular modifications (see Chapter 7), and using computers in the classroom, their attitudes changed again. By the end of the year, teachers felt students with behavior problems were the most difficult to include and they began working on a more stringent behavior management and counseling program for students with very challenging social behaviors (see Chapter 6).

Intermediate School

This intermediate school provided programs for students in the fifth and sixth grades. They used the Core Team concept wherein small groups of four teachers are clustered together in close teaching proximity and work as an instructional team. As a team they are responsible for a larger body of students who are rotated for instruction in language arts, mathematics, science, and social studies among the four teachers on the Core Team. This structure was already in place and the faculty was already accustomed to working in teams.

There was a self-contained, special education program for six students with severe disabilities in this school. This was the only such class at this level for the entire district and the six students came from across the district.

The principal was considered to be the most progressive and energetic principal in the district. He typically obtained more grant and special monies than any other principal in the district. Prior to leading this school to being more collaborative and inclusive, he was a member of the school district's vertical school team for study and training in inclusion provided by the state education agency.

The members of a vertical team represent people from all levels within the school system. This team created a philosophy that serves as a "draft philosophy" for educators throughout the district to consider and to provide input for possible refinement (see Chapter 3, Figure 3.1, for more information about this team's vision). Diversity among members was key to the vertical team, which was comprised of two building principals, a director of special education, a director of curriculum and instruction, an associate superintendent, some classroom teachers, some special education teachers, a parent of a student with disabilities, and a school counselor.

As a result of his work on the vertical team, this principal decided to offer 1.5 days of staff development in building collaborative and inclusive schools to the intermediate school faculty. When they came together for this training with me, the circumstances were difficult. The sessions took place on the days immediately preceding the beginning of the new school year, and the faculty would, frankly, have preferred to spend the time preparing for their classes. Another problem was that they had just received their class lists and many had just discovered they had one or more students with special education needs assigned to their class. Some were resentful and some were very concerned because they did not feel comfortable teaching and managing students with special needs. A third related problem was inequity in assignment of students with challenges to the various teachers. Some had none, others had too many!

After the training, this faculty made some important, collective decisions using the collaborative decision-making process (see Chapter 3). They decided there would be equity in assignment of students with challenges across all the classroom teachers. As a faculty they agreed that part of creating a collaborative school was to share the teaching load.

They also decided that much stress associated with inclusion would be relieved if the classroom teachers could have advance notice as to which students with special education needs would be assigned to their classes. They agreed that for students already in the school district, the receiving teacher for the following September would know in March of that same year who that student would be. This advance time would allow the teacher time to visit the student in his or her current classroom, meet with former teachers, parents, and the student, and plan for any accommodations that might be necessary.

The faculty included all students with mild and moderate learning and behavior problems in the general classes. They retained the self-contained class for students with severe and multiple handicaps.

High School

This school was an inner-city high school with a mission to provide academic and vocational/technical curricula and preparation for its students. The student body was primarily African American and Hispanic, with the grade levels ranging from 9th to 12th grade. The principal was an African American woman from the community who was familiar with community traditions and was viewed as a leader in the community and the school.

This principal and her faculty developed a specific plan of action to help the faculty in building a more collaborative and inclusive school. The Instructional Collaboration Action Plan was part of a proposal this faculty prepared to obtain state monies for developing an inclusion program and for funding related staff development opportunities. The plan of action they developed is displayed in Table 1.1.

The principal and the faculty made the decision to use a teacher assistance team to support classroom teachers who had special education students in their classes or who had students who were at risk and posed special challenges to the teacher. There was a preponderance of the latter. This team would be an additional type of support to classroom teachers (there was already an existing remedial reading program that students took as an elective course).

The principal decided that the department chairpersons should form the teacher assistance team. There were nine such people on the team. They attended 3 days of staff development for team training and developed their own plan of action for what needed to take place to implement the team. They decided to have rotating terms on the team, so that at any given point there would be a five-member team plus the referring classroom teacher. They decided to name this teacher assistance team "The Dream Team." The Dream Team would be available to all faculty members on an as-needed basis. The referring teacher in that respective department would be able to access the team through the department chairperson.

The department chairpersons and the principal also determined that each chairperson would conduct informal staff development sessions in the departmental meetings. This way the information the team received during training, especially specific strategies for adapting instruction and curriculum, could be shared with all faculty members in each department in an ongoing fashion. Using the existing administrative structure, the department chairpersons were held accountable for Dream Team interventions and ongoing staff development in the individual departments.

Summary

Each of these three schools is unique. In each example, the principal and faculty, including the special education faculty, worked together to create a vision of a collaborative and inclusive school. In essence, I supported them in viewing their school as a separate and unique culture—a culture that would utilize its existing resources to create a base for collaborative and inclusive schooling, and a culture that would expand from the base and create new options for instructional services to students in ways that would be most facilitative for the faculty and that would ensure implementation.

All three schools created vehicles for service delivery for both special education students and students at risk for school failure, making certain they provided for prevention, remediation, and coordination. All three schools created collaborative structures that would encourage and facilitate faculty and staff working together in teams

TABLE 1.1
Instructional Collaboration Action Plan

Specific steps/ activities	Resources/ budget	Responsible group/dept.	Date to implement	Progress
Self-development training in the collaborative process for modification of instruction for inclusive classes of students with varying skill levels and including all students with learning disabilities, behavior problems, language differences, physical differences, mild retardation, and at risk for school failure.	SBM Funds	P. Dungy & L. Idol	September 17–19, 1995	Ten faculty members spent 3 days in intensive staff development at Fort Worth Botanical Gardens
Present collaborative concept of instruction to entire faculty • overview of Dream Team process		T. Levy	September 25, 1996	Overview presented to all faculty/staff members
Ongoing publicity for the collaborative process • fliers (Dream Team/CORE Team guidelines) • weekly bulletin • testimonials • "true confessions" of referring teachers		P. Dungy	September, 1995	Dream Team recognized for training
Inform parents of referred students • letter that outlines instructional modifications as designed by the Dream Team • Parent Connection system to notify parents of meeting date and time		P. Dungy	January, 1996	
Departments • Complete "The Acid Test" inventory to describe teacher instructional expectations and student behaviors • May make universal lesson plans from instructional modifications • May develop lesson plans for a department file or packages of instructional modifications		Department Chairs	October department meetings	Reading, social studies, English, Language Center, vocational, math, and science departments have completed The Acid Test

(*continues*)

TABLE 1.1 *Continued.*

Specific steps/ activities	Resources/ budget	Responsible group/dept.	Date to implement	Progress
Teachers • Will identify and refer names of students who are not experiencing academic success and could gain from instructional modification		All Teachers	January, 1996	
Dream Team • Will meet twice monthly to focus on instructional collaboration utilizing the problem-solving process, pending the number of teacher referrals • Will develop a referral team that identifies the kind of problem, a quick reading assessment score, and strategies already used by the teacher • Will rotate individuals serving on the team • Will work with referring teachers to modify instruction for classes or individual students using the Model Lesson Plan from *Effective Instruction of Difficult-To-Teach Students* (Idol & West, 1993) • Will use the Collaborative Problem-Solving Worksheet (see Appendix 5.A) for students not achieving academic success • Will look for problems common to all teachers • Will rotate duties on the team • Will keep records of the numbers of teachers and students served • Will keep a binder of all modified lesson plans in the library for faculty use • Will periodically post a model lesson on the bulletin board in the workroom	$2,880 Low-Performing Grant	Dream Team Members	January, 1996	

of various sizes. And all three schools had very supportive principals who were viewed as instructional leaders. Finally, in all three schools the principal and the faculty made a conscious commitment to moving toward educating all students in the general education program.

In each of the schools, the faculty created the types of service delivery that would best meet their needs. In the elementary school it was a combination of consulting and cooperative teaching by the special educator, coupled with increased use of instructional assistants. In the intermediate school, it was with Core Teams, which assigned all students (with the exception of six with severe challenges) to general classroom instruction, controlling for the proportion of students with special needs in a given class, and giving teachers plenty of advance time to prepare for inclusion of a student with special needs in their classrooms. In the high school it was the Dream Team, a teacher assistance team created by a nine-member group of department chairpersons that was available to all faculty; this school also retained an existing remedial reading program.

The reader is cautioned not to conclude that the type of service delivery each school group chose is related to the level of schooling (i.e., elementary, intermediate, or high school). Any one of the various options used across the three schools could have been implemented at either of the other two levels if the faculty had chosen to do so. I have seen many instances of such cross-applications. Rather, the primary point is that each faculty worked as a collegial and collaborative group with strong leadership to create the service delivery options that would be best for them.

In all three schools, it was accepted that change comes about when a vision is created, that all are expected to adhere to the vision, and that the change will be gradual, planned, and evaluated. Key to our understanding of what happened in these schools is understanding that the changes that were made were school-wide changes that involved everyone, both in decision making and in implementation.

CHAPTER TWO

◆ ◆

What Does It Mean for a School To Be Collaborative?

◆ A common theme among the three schools described in Chapter 1 is that collaboration among education professionals, parents, and students is highly valued. The exemplar schools described in Chapter 1 have in common several characteristics. The self- and group-consensual ratings of each school faculty on an instrument such as the one in Appendix 2.A would be relatively high, with several indicators that the staff members are collegial and value the team approach to problem resolution. (You are advised to read through this chapter and then use the instrument in Appendix 2.A as a means of helping determine how collaborative your school is.)

Characteristics of the Collaborative School

Because the collaborative school is a composite of beliefs and practices, it is easier to describe than to define. Perhaps the best way to characterize the collaborative school is to list its elements, as identified by Smith and Scott (1990):

- the belief, based on effective school research, that the quality of education is largely determined by what happens at the school site;

- the conviction, also supported by research findings, that instruction is most effective in a school environment characterized by norms of collegiality and continual improvement;

- the belief that teachers are professionals who should be given responsibility for the instructional process and held accountable for its outcomes;

- the use of a wide range of practices and structures that enable administrators and teachers to work together on school improvement;

- the involvement of teachers in decisions about school goals and the means for achieving them.

Implicit in these elements is the overriding goal of the collaborative school: education improvement. Although a host of other benefits may be expected to derive from collaboration—staff harmony, mutual respect among teachers and administrators, and a professional work environment for teachers—its primary rationale is the instructional effectiveness that results when teachers participate collegially in school improvement and in their own professional growth.

The Collaborative Consultation Model

The Collaborative Consultation Model has been instrumental in building a sound base for helping school staffs develop more collaborative schools (Idol, Nevin, & Paolucci-Whitcomb, 1994), as well as helping staff members develop program planning. In order to use the Collaborative Consultation Model effectively, members of any problem-solving group in the collaborative school should have expertise in the following three areas: (a) an underlying knowledge base, (b) collaborative problem solving and communicative/interactive skills, and (c) positive intrapersonal attitudes. Refer to Figure 2.1 for a depiction of how these areas of professional development influence collaborative consultation. The intersecting circles in Figure 2.1 represent three collaborators (C1, C2, C3) working together on a common (T=targeted) problem. The circles are of equal size to indicate that all collaborators are of equal status in the problem-solving process.

More specifically, the underlying knowledge base for collaborative consultation is what I have defined as the scientific base of consultation, which is the content or knowledge base the collaborator brings to the collaborative problem-solving process (Idol, 1990, p. 5). This knowledge is comprised of a wide span of content pertaining to the technical aspects of program implementation and includes techniques in assessment, instructional interventions, curricular and materials modifications and adapta-

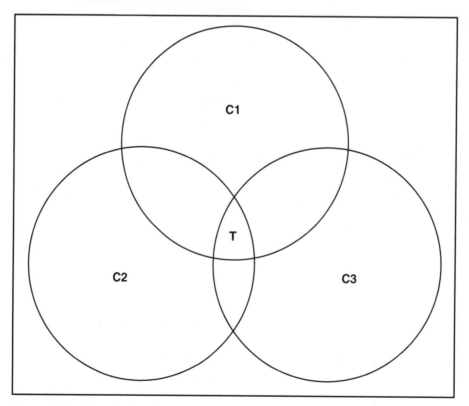

Figure 2.1 The collaborative consultation model.

TABLE 2.1

Essential Components of the Underlying Knowledge Base

Module	Component
1	Elements of effective instruction
2	Effective instructional decision making
3	Student portfolio assessment
4	Curriculum-based student assessment
5	Observation of instructional environments
6	Strategic and cognitive instruction
7	Curriculum adaptation
8	Instruction adaptation
9	Education materials evaluation and selection
10	Effective classroom management and discipline
11	Management of the teaching and learning environment
12	Student progress evaluation

Note. Adapted from *Effective Instruction of Difficult-To-Teach Students*, by L. Idol and J. F. West, 1993, Austin, TX: PRO-ED.

tions, and classroom and student management (see Chapters 7 and 8 for more detailed descriptions).

More interventions related to effective inclusion and the underlying knowledge base of teachers can be found in various chapters in Idol et al. (1994) and in a staff development curriculum (Idol & West, 1993) comprised of the 12 modules listed in Table 2.1. Selection of the modular topics was based on an extensive interdisciplinary research review of effective instruction in inclusive classrooms coupled with a Delphi-panel voting process. The panel members represented many different strata of American education and came from most of the states in the United States (West & Cannon, 1988).

The second area of expertise—interpersonal communicative, interactive, and problem-solving skills—represents the kinds of behaviors collaborators may use to enhance the problem-solving process. I have described this "the artful base of consultation" elsewhere as follows: "The artful base is basically the way in which collaborators work with one another to solve problems. This base consists of the process skills of consultation. It is a demonstrable knowledge of how to bring about effective decision making, how to solve problems with others, and how to interact and communicate effectively with others" (Idol, 1990, p. 5).

In the Collaborative Consultation Model, these various types of skills are described as principles to be practiced by effective collaborators. Table 2.2 is a listing of some of the overriding principles of collaborative consultation that may enhance the collaborative process. These principles are thought to be so pervasive to the collaborative process that they are relevant in any of the stages of problem solving (described in Chapter 3).

The intrapersonal attitudes described in the Collaborative Consultation Model reflect the personal behaviors that each collaborator brings to the group process. As suggested by Gardner (1993), intrapersonal intelligence is an important aspect of the concept of multiple intelligences. These beliefs, values, and experiences are unique to

TABLE 2.2

Principles of Collaborative Consultation

1. Establish informal relationships among team members prior to beginning professional work.

2. Treat all team members with respect.

3. Use situational leadership to guide the group, adjusting the leadership style to the needs of the group.

4. Learn to manage conflict and confrontation effectively.

5. Be willing to share information and create a trustworthy relationship so others feel safe to share.

6. Listen actively when others are speaking.

7. Engage in nonjudgmental responding when sharing ideas.

8. Use appropriate interviewing skills for gaining and sharing information; expressing and discovering feelings; planning for action; problem solving.

9. Use appropriate and jargon-free language for both oral and written communication.

10. Gather practical and useful data and information to aid in decision making.

11. Be willing to both give and receive feedback from team members.

12. Always remember to give others credit for their ideas and accomplishments.

13. Be aware of nonverbal messages, so that positive signals are given.

Note. Adapted from *Collaborative Consultation* (2nd ed.), by L. Idol, P. Paolucci-Whitcomb, and A. Nevin, 1994, Austin, TX: PRO-ED.

each individual, yet impact upon the group process. Table 2.3 contains some specific attitudinal statements that may serve as a guide to each collaborator in the development of a personal set of self-preservation and survival skills that may lead to self-enhancement and growth, as well as have a positive impact on the collaborative group. These intrapersonal attitudes are explained in more detail in Chapter 10.

It is my recommendation that any group of professionals interested in using the Collaborative Consultation Model ensure that prospective collaborators have developed skills in each of these three areas. Collaborators can conduct self-assessments in each of these areas to determine which, if any, are in need of improvement (see Chapter 9 for a self-assessment instrument on effective communication and Chapter 10 for self-assessment of attitudes and beliefs pertaining to inclusion). Additional needs assessment instruments and related staff development materials on collaborative problem solving and communicative/interactive skills, as well as on some of the intrapersonal attitudes, can be found in West, Idol, and Cannon (1989); see Idol and West (1993) for the underlying knowledge bases.

Is Your School Collaborative?

Refer to Appendix 2.A to assess how collaborative you and your faculty think your school is. It is important that each individual use the assessment instrument, and then for the large group to discuss the findings. If your group is very large, it will be better

TABLE 2.3

Intrapersonal Attitudes Relevant to Collaborative Consultation

1. Face fear
2. Share a sense of humor
3. Behave with integrity
4. Live with joy
5. Take risks
6. Use self-determination
7. Think longitudinally
8. Create new norms
9. Respond proactively
10. Adapt upward
11. Use self-differentiation

Note. From *Collaborative Consultation* (2nd ed., p. 33), by L. Idol, A. Nevin, and P. Paolucci-Whitcomb, 1994, Austin, TX: PRO-ED. Copyright 1994 by PRO-ED. Reprinted with permission.

to have small-group discussions, with a group spokesperson chosen to report the general impressions to the larger group. A large group facilitator can compile the general ratings reported by the small-group spokespersons. This is a good method for building consensus among members of a large group, while at the same time ensuring that individual perceptions and ideas are recognized and valued.

After consensus is reached on the general impressions of the entire group, those areas needing further development can be identified. It is important to include these targeted areas in the annual school improvement plan so the areas are truly addressed and the need to improve is endorsed by the entire group.

Summary

I have explored the basic tenets of what it means for a school faculty to be collaborative. The Collaborative Consultation Model (see Figure 2.1), coupled with the group's consensual assessment, is the primary base for determining where your group is. Understanding and applying each of the three dimensions in the triangle of this model will do much to prepare team members for collaboration.

APPENDIX 2.A
How Collaborative Is Your School?

Name _____ Position _____

School/Unit _____ Date _____

Directions: It is recommended that faculty groups complete this self-assessment. Please read each statement carefully. Next rate the degree to which each statement reflects the current work environment in your school, using the scale listed below. Then discuss the findings with the others in your group, reaching consensus on the overall impressions of the group.

1 = our staff members always behave this way
2 = our staff members behave this way most of the time
3 = our staff members behave this way sometimes
4 = our staff members behave this way rarely
5 = our staff members never behave this way

_____ 1. The staff members share a common language about instructional techniques.

_____ 2. The staff often observe one another in their classrooms and give one another feedback.

_____ 3. The staff frequently discuss instructional techniques and methods in the staff workroom or lounge.

_____ 4. The staff work together to master new instructional methods or strategies.

_____ 5. The staff plan and design educational materials together.

_____ 6. The staff pool their expertise and share their resources with one another.

_____ 7. The staff learn from and with each other.

_____ 8. Time is specifically devoted at staff meetings to demonstrating and discussing new or innovative educational techniques, materials, or strategies.

_____ 9. Discussions in the faculty lounge center mostly on instructional practices rather than on social concerns or complaints about students.

_____ 10. Time is specifically provided for professional staff to plan and problem solve collaboratively.

Note. Adapted from *Collaborative School: What! So What! Now What!*, by P. Roy and P. O'Brien, 1989, November, paper presented at the Annual Conference of the National Staff Development Council, Anaheim, CA. Copyright 1989 by P. Roy and P. O'Brien. Adapted with permission.

CHAPTER THREE

◆ ◆ ◆ ◆ ◆ ◆ ◆ ◆ ◆ ◆ ◆ ◆ ◆ ◆ ◆ ◆ ◆ ◆

What Does It Mean for a School To Be Inclusive?

◆ In this chapter, 15 key questions that I have found to be helpful to educators in building inclusive and collaborative schools are set forth and explored. The questions emerged as a result of my work as an education consultant in the United States, Canada, Australia, and New Zealand. Despite some international and regional differences in how schooling is offered, these 15 questions seem to be basic and relevant to any school district or division interested in collaborative and inclusive schooling.

The 15 questions are divided into three categories. The first category addresses questions of a more general and philosophical nature. The second category deals with some of the practical mechanics of inclusion, such as parental support, funding, adequate support of teachers, and descriptions of various types of service delivery options. The third category addresses practical implementation issues, such as provision of time to collaborate, job role clarifications, making certain collaborative teams know how to work together, ensuring that teachers know what to implement in the classrooms, student disciplinary practices, teacher resistance, preparing all students for inclusion, and program monitoring.

General and Philosophical Questions

1. Has Inclusion Been Defined Collaboratively?

As discussed in Chapter 1, inclusion occurs when a student with special learning or behavioral needs is educated full time in the general education program. Special education has a long and storied history of valuing the individual child, and this care and consideration is still applied in collaborative and inclusive schools today.

It is critical for school districts and divisions to create opportunities for groups of professionals to work together in a collaborative manner to determine whether inclusion is the best choice for a student with disabilities and to develop a workable classroom program. The group, not an individual educator, also should determine if academic or social inclusion, or a specific combination of both, is more appropriate. It is very important for inclusion decisions to be made on a child-by-child basis by teams of professionals and parents working together. When this is not done, problems with

---

This chapter is an extended version of an address given by the author at the International Council for Exceptional Children in April 1994, published in Idol (1994b) and adapted from Idol (1997a).

discrepancies among individual team members arise as to what appropriate inclusion really is. Such decisions should never be made on a programmatic basis, such as "All students in the inclusion program will get the following. . . ." Rather, each student with special education needs should first be considered an individual with rights: a right to be treated equitably and a right to the fullest educational experience possible. This kind of thinking falls in line well with the thoughts behind the Individuals with Disabilities Education Act (IDEA) and its predecessor, the Education for All Handicapped Children Act of 1975.

A modified continuum of services housed within the confines of the collaborative school is a reasonable and responsible approach to the inclusion problem (see also Vaughn & Schumm, 1995). This continuum should include neighborhood schooling for all children (even for those with the most profound and severe challenges); a self-contained special education classroom with heavy emphasis on mainstreaming; a supportive resource program; a special education consulting teacher program; a special education cooperative teaching program; and use of a building-based team(s) to consult with classroom teachers for any classroom problem.

This type of modified continuum speaks well to Fuchs and Fuchs' (1994) call for the need to redefine the relationship between special and general education. Specifically, they called for recognizing the need for change, appreciating the importance of consensus building, looking at general education with a sense of what is possible, respecting special education's traditions and values and the law that undergirds them, and seeking to strengthen the mainstream, as well as other educational options. In my consulting experiences with school systems, this is precisely what the majority is trying to achieve.

2. Has the School District Developed a Philosophical Position on Inclusion?

This is one of the most important, and most often overlooked, steps to take in building collaborative and inclusive schools. Schools sometimes neglect the collaborative process as they develop their philosophical position, with only certain individuals or a single individual developing a philosophy and imposing it on others. Some individuals within the district will feel as if the philosophy has been mandated or imposed upon them, rather than it having emerged from a collective effort. Because the philosophy has been generated by only a few individuals, the majority of the educational staff members are not likely to feel ownership. In this case, conflicting individual perceptions regarding the district's position on inclusion are likely to proliferate. This in turn results in sending mixed and inconsistent messages to the community, to teachers, and to administrators within the system.

Most school districts and divisions are in a state of flux because they have no district philosophy on inclusion. As often happens, the people at the administrative levels wait for the principals and teachers to develop the practice first, and the latter wait and, sometimes, hope for the direction to come from central administration. Instead, it is recommended that both groups work together to create a philosophical position that reflects what the collective group wants to create and offer to students.

Figure 3.1 contains an example of one philosophical position that was originally developed by a vertical school team, meaning that its members represented people

PHILOSOPHY OF INCLUSION

The philosophy of the Nacogdoches Independent School District is to ensure that all children, regardless of disability, cultural background, or socioeconomic status, have available to them the appropriate resources, services, and support necessary to meet their unique individual and educational needs. The district will continually strive to provide the best educational services available because of its students. The school and community will function as a family to nurture and support educational and social needs of everyone.

Figure 3.1. Statement of a philosophy of inclusion.

from all levels within the school system. This team is in the same school district as the intermediate school described in Chapter 1. This team created a philosophy that then served as a "draft philosophy" for educators throughout the district to consider and to provide input for possible refinement. Key to its inception was that the philosophy was created by a group of people. The team was comprised of two building principals (one was the principal of the intermediate school described in Chapter 1), a director of special education, a director of curriculum and instruction, an associate superintendent, several classroom teachers, several special education teachers, a parent of a student with disabilities, and a school counselor. This is not a prescription for who should comprise such a vertical team, but rather a description of a single vertical team. Each group should decide for itself who is best to serve on the team.

The Nacogdoches, Texas, philosophical statement in Figure 3.1 is provided solely as an example of a school district's philosophical position. It is the result of several drafts that each went through the consensus-building process until reaching its present state. An earlier draft actually contained stronger wording advocating inclusionary practices. Its present form represents a consensual position of the district personnel and was presented to the school board for its approval at the writing of this chapter. The purpose in presenting it here is definitely *not* for readers to reproduce it and/or implement it with their school group. The actual process of collaboratively developing such a document is crucial to the change effort. It is one thing to read something others have created; it is quite another to be a part of a group creating a philosophical stand to which everyone can adhere, morally and professionally. In this way, the philosophical position becomes an integral part of the school culture.

3. What Are the Attitudes and Beliefs of the Teachers Toward Inclusion?

An important element in bringing about effective change is to provide and build a collegial atmosphere for supporting teachers in sharing their intrapersonal attitudes and beliefs. It is simply not enough to hope negative attitudes and beliefs will go away or to hope the more positive attitudes and beliefs will influence others over time. People need safe professional environments (collaborative teams, pairs of teachers, faculty gatherings) where these attitudes and beliefs can be explored, shared, challenged, restructured, rethought, and so forth. If negative attitudes are kept under wraps in a repressive atmosphere, these attitudes are likely to corrode the change effort, spreading in an undercover, contagious fashion throughout the staff.

TABLE 3.1

Common Types of Resistance of Teachers Toward Inclusion

- Classroom teachers who are accustomed to referring students for alternative placement when they experience difficulty in the classroom

- Special education and remedial teachers who are overly protective of special education students, believing they are the only appropriate teachers for them

- Teachers focusing on the size of the class and the unfairness to the other students by treating one student differently

- Teachers focusing on the family as the "cause" of the problem

- Teachers believing that every single student in a classroom should function at the curricular grade level, even though this is never actually the case

- Teachers focusing on influencing variables beyond teacher's/school's control (e.g., alcoholic or drug-dependent family, low socioeconomic status, lowered morals of family, dysfunctional families, uncooperative parents)

- Teachers believing students with moderate and severe disabilities must be paired with an adult at all times

- Faculty and staff being afraid they will injure students with physical disabilities

- Faculty and staff lacking experience and time with people with disabilities

---

Table 3.1 lists some of the most frequently occurring reasons that teachers resist inclusion. These reasons have been revealed when the ambience in staff development sessions is such that people can share comfortably some of their concerns. The reasons seem to arise regardless of locale, country, or state. In my experience, however, one national difference appears to be that educators in the United States seem more concerned than educators in Australia, New Zealand, and Canada that all students receive all instructional content in a single grade level.

Another key factor in creating the proper atmosphere for sharing attitudes and beliefs is that interdisciplinary groups work through these issues together. It is best that these groups include principals, classroom teachers, special and remedial teachers, inclusion specialists, school psychologists and counselors, social workers, speech–language specialists, physical therapists, parents, and so forth (see Chapter 10 for a more in-depth exploration of the attitudes and beliefs that influence successful inclusion).

Mechanics of Inclusion Questions

4. Does the District Have Parental Support of Inclusion?

It is important to the development of inclusion programs that a task force of parents and educators serve in an advisory capacity to the district. Taking a planned and proactive stance is highly preferable to offering inclusion in defense to parental pressure. Sometimes, school groups build inclusion programs because certain parents of children with special education challenges are making demands that their children be included.

This reactionary stance often results in school districts making inclusion an option, but it is in the form of defense. Rather, the development of inclusion programs should be proactive, with time and consideration given to each of the questions described in this article, allowing time for staff to develop quality programs rather than reactionary ones.

In many school districts parents are split on the issue of inclusion. Some want to have their children educated separately and some want them to be included. In this situation, I have seen districts give parents an either/or option of placing their students in integrated or segregated programs, with neither option being proactively developed. This "divided" approach to the issue is a concern because it is usually adopted in lieu of developing a district philosophy regarding inclusion. Consequently, it often results in split and divisive thinking in communities, rather than in a communal approach to the education of children with exceptionalities and challenges.

It is important to develop an effective parental support system by making a conscious effort to inform and involve parents. This effort involves soliciting parental input and feedback and inviting parents to school to observe and participate in program development.

5. Does the District Have the Money To Offer Inclusion Programs?

Responsible inclusion programs are expensive. A responsible program includes offering classroom teachers a variety of support systems for effective instruction of difficult-to-teach students (see also Question 6). Some districts offer inclusion programs because it's the morally right position to take, but they do not engage in adequate long-term financial planning. Some district administrators offer inclusion because it is thought to be less expensive than segregation, reasoning that fewer support staff will be needed. Some districts and some individual schools are achieving better cost accommodations in a variety of ways. Some of these are as follows:

A. Build community/business/school partnerships, with the partners donating money and services to the programs.

B. Reconsider how support staff are funded and move to cross-funding staff positions so that support staff services can be offered to a variety of students in a classroom.

C. Use some local tax dollars to fund parts of programs, rather than relying exclusively on state and federal special education funds or on temporary grant monies.

D. Reconsider how current funds are being used. For example, in one school the principal decided to stop using Title I monies (federal monies for remedial programs for students with disadvantages) to fund pull-out teacher positions and instead used the monies to fund instructional assistants. In that school, with the combination of special education monies and Title I federal monies, they now have an instructional assistant for every two classroom teachers (see Chapter 1).

E. Utilize special project monies, if they are available, for schools that want to develop innovative practices for students at risk for school failure or for developing effective inclusion programs.

F. Use site-based decision making, where a team of teachers and the principal make decisions about how resource monies will be used in the building.

In nearly all instances, some reconsideration of how funds are used is a necessary part of developing and offering inclusion programs. Involving people in the decision-making processes of how funds will be used, created, or co-created empowers them. Empowered people create impressive instructional programs when they become committed to building collaborative and inclusive schools. And decision making about monies is a powerful form of commitment.

6. How Are All Teachers Being Supported To Offer Inclusion Programs?

Teachers must be supported in a variety of ways if they are to react to inclusion favorably. One very important way is to offer comprehensive professional development opportunities in essential areas such as (a) effective instruction of difficult-to-teach students in general education programs; (b) developing collaborative skills in communicating, interacting, problem solving, and team decision making; (c) key issues in program development and implementation; and (d) exploring, sharing, and reconciling intrapersonal attitudes and beliefs related to inclusion. Comprehensive professional development also includes opportunities for teachers to use peer coaching—teaching and providing feedback to one another about the teaching and learning process in inclusive classrooms.

An integral part of offering support to teachers is making a conscious effort to build a truly collegial staff, as indicated in the extensive literature on effective schooling. This often means that the entire staff needs training opportunities in how to work in collegial and collaborative teams. Once this is accomplished, the entire staff should define and agree on which of the various service delivery options for offering inclusion programs will be used.

7. How Many Ways Is Service Delivery Provided To Support Inclusion?

Some school districts use only one way of providing supportive special education service delivery to classroom teachers. In my experience this singular approach is simply not sufficient. A combined program that includes several options for offering instructional support to classroom teachers often works best because (a) not everyone feels comfortable with the same service delivery option and (b) a single option may not provide equal support for all grade levels or all classes.

The essential service delivery options for supporting inclusive classrooms and teachers include cooperative teaching (e.g., Bauwens & Hourcade, 1995; Bauwens, Hourcade, & Friend, 1989); consulting teaching (e.g., Idol, 1989, 1993; Idol et al., 1994); instructional assistants in the classroom (e.g., Welch, Richards, Okada, Richards, & Prescott, 1995); and teams of teachers providing planning and problem-solving assistance to classroom teachers (e.g., Chalfant & Van Dusen Pysh, 1989; Saver & Downes, 1990). These four models of service delivery are defined in Table 3.2 and explored in considerable detail in Chapter 4.

The final selection of the most appropriate combination of options for a particular school should result in offering programming at each of at least three levels of intervention: prevention of learning and behavioral problems, remediation of learning and behavioral problems, and coordination of instructional programs. School groups are

TABLE 3.2

Definitions of Various Service Delivery Options for Supporting Classroom Teachers

Cooperative teaching	A support staff teacher, usually a special education teacher, teaches collaboratively with the classroom teacher in the general classroom.
Consulting teaching	A consulting teacher works as a collaborative classroom consultant to a classroom teacher. This teacher does not work directly with students but rather serves as consultant, collaboratively planning, assessing, and developing materials and instructional and curricular modifications with the classroom teacher. Sometimes, shared demonstration teaching is done on a short-term, modeling and developmental basis.
Instructional assistants	A para-professional assistant assists the classroom teacher with instruction and is supervised by the classroom teacher and/or consulting teacher.
Teacher assistance teams	A team of teachers (classroom and support teachers) serves as a consulting body to a referring classroom teacher. The referring teacher joins the team and the team develops a specific plan of action for intervention with student-, instructional-, classroom management-, student discipline-, and curricular-related problems.

encouraged to have at least one service delivery option for supporting classroom teachers at each of these three levels.

Implementation of Inclusion Questions

8. Are Faculty Provided With Sufficient Time To Collaborate?

The most frequently indicated barrier for why school faculties cannot work together collaboratively is lack of time to meet. Sufficient time must be provided for professional collaboration. Faculty members should not be expected to do their collaborative planning and decision making during curriculum planning/preparation time or before and after school. It is a prerequisite in any profession that professionals within that field need time to consult with one another. Should the professional educator expect less?

West and Idol (1990, p. 30), in conducting field visitations, identified 11 different solutions to the time problem, implemented by various school faculties, with the support of their principal. Each of these is a means of releasing a classroom teacher for a small amount of time so that that teacher can work with a consulting teacher, a cooperative teacher, or a teacher assistance team. These solutions are listed in the first part of Table 3.3. The second part of Table 3.3 contains some additional strategies that I have learned from working with various school groups in recent years. Each of the various solutions is designed to be used for relatively brief periods of time (e.g., approximately 30 minutes).

9. Does Everybody Know What They Are Supposed To Do?

Staff must collectively define the various adult roles involved in the inclusive and collaborative effort. Problems arise when there are discrepant ideas as to what the roles

TABLE 3.3

No-Cost or Low-Cost Strategies for Increasing Teachers' Consultation Time

Strategies Reported by Idol and West (1991)

- Regularly bring large groups of students together for special types of experiences (e.g., films, guest speakers, plays, etc.).

- The principal and other support staff teach a period a day on a regularly scheduled basis.

- When students are doing independent projects/study, arrange for them to be clustered together in larger groups (e.g., in the library or multipurpose room) with fewer supervising staff.

- Hire a permanent "floating" substitute teacher (this teacher rotates across the various classrooms; some schools use two part-time substitutes so that two teachers can be released at once; some use Community/School Partnerships to pay for this cost).

- Utilize cross-age or same-age peer tutors with fewer supervising staff.

- Utilize volunteers (e.g., parents, grandparents, community/business leaders, retired teachers) to supervise in classes.

- The principal assigns a specific time each day or week for collaboration only.

- Alter the school day for teachers, without students, on a regular basis.

- Utilize student teachers who are offering lessons approved by master teachers.

- The principal sets aside one day per grading period designated as "collaboration day" (no other activities can be substituted on this day).

- Obtain a faculty consensus to extend the instructional day for 20 minutes 2 days per week to provide a collaboration period for staff (days and times can be staggered to free staff at different times).

Additional Solutions from Recent Site Visits and Staff Development Sessions

- When teachers are on maternity leave, invite them to return for occasional, brief teaching stints.

- Rotate assignments for playground or duty assignments so there are times when individual faculty will collaborate instead of taking a duty.

- Make collaboration time a priority and a legality by including it in an included student's Individual Education Program (IEP).

- Rotate principals, assistant principals, and deputies across classrooms for occasional relief.

- Utilize central office administrative and supervisory staff to do occasional teaching stints.

- Utilize counselors, nurses, and computer lab teachers to teach specialty enrichment classes for brief and occasional instructional periods.

- Use parent volunteers to teach brief units on study skills or to teach the students a specialty that parent has to offer.

- Utilize instructional assistants to relieve teachers.

of one another are among school staff. For example, if planning for consultative services is not done on a school-wide basis, ill feelings and misunderstandings are bound to result.

Some real examples include (a) concluding that consulting teachers are not really doing their jobs because they are seen walking in the halls from class to class and are not working directly with students; (b) concluding that members of the teacher assistance team have some type of special status with the principal because they are released from their classes to do their team work; (c) instructional assistants quitting their jobs because they thought they would be doing clerical assistance work and they find themselves being expected to work directly with students; or (d) classroom teachers being upset because they think they will be responsible for assisting a student with severe physical handicaps with toileting needs.

An important strategy in overcoming these misperceptions is for the faculty to work together to define what the job roles will be for any new or modified positions created. Often during faculty retreats, in faculty inservice sessions, and in faculty planning meetings, a co-working atmosphere emerges. It usually occurs when the faculty has the opportunity to "brainstorm" the ways they believe the particular job should look and then reach consensus on a reasonable refinement of those ideas. Occasionally, faculty do this by each member making a private list and then feeding these responses to the site-based management team, which refines a master list and returns it to the faculty for additional feedback and refinement. These job descriptions also seem to be constantly under revision, as faculty experiment with new ways of conducting these roles and make ongoing changes and refinements, using a Discrepancy Evaluation Model (Provus, 1971; see Idol et al., 1994, for a description).

Each school group should create its own unique job descriptions. This is very important if groups are to take school-wide ownership of the job creations and develop their own unique collaborative and inclusive school. Examples of what some of these creations look like can be found in Chapter 4. These should not be reproduced verbatim and simply mandated. Successful implementation will not occur this way; rather, ownership occurs when groups work together collaboratively to create what best fits their own unique situations. Every school is best viewed as a separate culture, with its own values, mores, acceptable practices, and philosophies. Each group should create its own culture; this is how empowerment really occurs.

10. Do Teams and Pairs Know How To Work Together?

Certain identifiable skills (West & Cannon, 1988) are necessary in order to work effectively on a collaborative team, be it planning, teaching, decision making, evaluating, and so on. Comprehensive staff development in the areas of effective communication, team interaction, and team decision-making skills is an important first step in preparing staff for inclusion.

Teachers need team training in these skills during staff development sessions. The training should involve demonstration, simulated practice, and instructor and team member feedback. Emphasis should be placed on teaching a multiple-step problem-

LIBRARY
UNIVERSITY OF ST. FRANCIS
JOLIET, ILLINOIS

solving process. An example is the six-step, collaborative process described by Idol et al. (1994):

- ◆ **Step 1:** Goal/Entry
- ◆ **Step 2:** Problem Identification
- ◆ **Step 3:** Intervention Recommendations
- ◆ **Step 4:** Intervention Plan of Action
- ◆ **Step 5:** Evaluation
- ◆ **Step 6:** Follow-up and Redesign

Once teams have learned this process, a more in-depth opportunity can be provided for improving communication and group interaction skills. During this time, supportive coaching can be provided to support individual team members in improving their skills; this can be coupled with individuals setting their own personal improvement goals.

Effective and efficient team collaborators need school follow-up visits. A consultant or outside observer can give feedback on the group problem-solving process and offer suggestions for refining and speeding up the collaborative process. In my experience as a consultant, teams use a structured worksheet to guide them through the collaborative problem-solving process and keep them attuned to the problem-solving task. An example of a commonly used worksheet is in West et al. (1989) and Appendix 5.A of this book.

11. Do the Faculty Know What To Do in the Classrooms?

Sometimes faculty are unsure of what to do to accommodate and include challenged students in the inclusive classroom. The answer to this question lies in a combination of a relevant assessment of staff development needs, related and relevant staff development, and the offering of various kinds of support to the teacher. The needs assessment can be of faculty strengths and weaknesses in planning, assessing, teaching, disciplining, managing the instructional environment, making materials and instructional modifications, and evaluating progress (see Idol & West, 1993).

Most often, faculty members possess much of the needed expertise. It is necessary to plan professional development, sharing teaching and coaching opportunities so that faculty can teach and learn from one another. Sometimes, modeling, demonstration teaching, and/or coaching in the classroom are all that are needed for inclusive instructional programs to be implemented. Much can be done collaboratively among the faculty members themselves with less reliance on outside consultants (see Chapters 7 and 8 for a discussion of instructional strategies to use in inclusive classrooms, including instructional adaptations, multi-layered lessons, and use of cooperative learning groups).

12. Is An Effective School-Wide Discipline Plan in Place?

Having an effective school-wide discipline plan is essential to responsible inclusion. Students who are not well disciplined are often not learning, are sometimes preventing others from learning, and are sometimes creating havoc in classrooms—all of which results in frustrated classroom teachers who are too overwhelmed to even consider inclusion on top of the chaos.

This school-wide discipline plan should include the following:

1. Listing six to eight positively stated behaviors of acceptable conduct for students. These are often listed in a Student Discipline Handbook.

2. Previewing acceptable conduct behaviors at the beginning of the school year with each class of students, and discussing what these expectations mean.

3. Signing the Student Discipline Management Contract; each student and the parents/guardians should sign and return the contract to the school.

4. Describing the consequences for school disruptions and failure to comply with the conduct standards in the Student Discipline Handbook.

5. Making the Student Discipline Handbook available to all students and their families.

6. Treating all students equally by expecting that all students in the school, regardless of disabling condition, meet these conduct standards. For special education students with conduct disorders, the Individualized Education Program (IEP) should include a plan for how to support the student in complying with these standards. Such students should not be exempted from adhering to the school-wide code of conduct. The reader is also referred to Chapter 6 for a discussion of various ways to accommodate students with behavioral problems in inclusive classrooms.

13. Are Faculty or Parents Particularly Resistant To Including Students With Certain Types of Disabilities?

Sometimes, adults possess particular beliefs and prejudices toward certain kinds of disabilities. These may be due to lack of exposure, ignorance, or past experiences. Creating an ambience that is conducive to sharing these fears and feelings is critical. Most often, when teachers are asked which types of students are the most difficult to include, their responses vary by individual and their experiences and beliefs.

Many teachers agree that students who are troubled or troubling are particularly challenging to include because of classroom disruption. (This speaks poignantly to Question 12, regarding an effective discipline plan used at a school-wide level.) Regarding this point, no student should be included in a general classroom who is a danger to him- or herself, to the teacher, or to other students in the class. Teachers and students have the right to teach and learn in safe environments and should be protected on this issue.

14. Are the Other Students in the Inclusive Classroom Prepared?

The other students in the class where inclusion is to take place must be educated in a healthy, positive, and nurturing way about the disability challenges of the included student. Generally, students are less resistant to inclusion than some adults, particularly those adults who have had no life experiences with people with disabilities. Children are naturally kind, unless they learn otherwise, and can be incredibly supportive of one another, especially under firm, positive, and strong teacher leadership.

In inclusive classrooms, teachers find they have to set parameters for how other students can help the student with special needs. Peers can be overly helpful. Many teachers use a buddy system, where selected peers are assigned to be a friend to a student who is included.

Sometimes teachers are very concerned that the student to be included creates an "unfair" environment in the classroom. This usually happens with a student who needs modifications in both curriculum and instruction. Often the teacher assumes such modifications would be unfair to other students. Teachers always have the right to set the classroom parameters. Students with IEPs have the right to appropriate modifications that will support them to learn in the most educational-enhancing environment possible. To provide such support to a special student does not have to mean that inequities be created. A relevant analogy is if one student requires crutches, can the provision of crutches to that student be afforded only when crutches are given to all classroom students? Providing teachers with exercises in such logical reasoning is a good way to help them work through some of their own thoughts and, sometimes, faulty conclusions.

Many times, teachers simply need to be empowered to make these adjustments for individual students, because somehow they have concluded that the most important value in general education is that all students have to be doing exactly the same thing at exactly the same time. Such a statement will not be written in any school district policy handbook, nor will administrative leaders espouse this belief, yet often teachers assume it. It is, however, important to prepare students for situations where an included student would have modifications in curriculum, instruction, discipline, assignments, or grading. When this approach is taken, students learn to care for others and they learn that all students are expected to work to their fullest potential, but that potentials do vary across individuals . . . this is a fact of life.

15. Do You Have a Monitoring Plan?

Ongoing and responsive evaluation is an integral part of building inclusive and collaborative schools. There are three classes of variables necessary in gathering evaluation data, including the following:

- *Student Change*—changes in skills, behaviors, and attitudes of students who are included and peers in the inclusion classroom

- *Adult Change*—changes in skills, behaviors, and attitudes of the adults involved in supporting the student to be included

- *System Change*—changes in school-based procedures, policies, instructional arrangements, school and classroom management, referrals to special programs, community support and attitudes, etc.

Some other important variables are numbers and types of students being educated in and out of the general education program; numbers of and types of referrals to special education per year; types of problems solved by the collaborative teams; the impact of the inclusion on other students; the impact of inclusion on the community; changes in intrapersonal attitudes and beliefs among educators; students, and parents; changes in the knowledge base of the faculty; and changes in collaborative skills of the faculty.

Summary

Responsible and effective inclusion does not occur because it is right or because it might cost less. Pressures from interest groups cannot mandate effective inclusion. It results only when people work together collaboratively and build a collective vision of what they want from inclusion. The 15 questions in this chapter are some basic ones that may be helpful in building a sound and proactive base for collaborative and inclusive schooling. The creation of schools where all children in a neighborhood have the right to learn to the maximum extent possible and where all teachers have the right to be supported in building collaborative and inclusive programs is imperative. See Appendix 3.A for a reproducible checklist of these 15 questions.

APPENDIX 3.A
A Checklist for Determining Degree of Implementation of a Collaborative and Inclusive School

Directions: For each item, indicate with a Yes or a No whether the question has been addressed.

_____ 1. Has inclusion been defined collaboratively?

_____ 2. Has the school district developed a philosophical position on inclusion?

_____ 3. What are the attitudes and beliefs of the teachers toward inclusion?

_____ 4. Does the district have parental support of inclusion?

_____ 5. Does the district have the money to offer inclusion programs?

_____ 6. How are all teachers being supported to offer inclusion programs?

_____ 7. How many ways is service delivery provided to support inclusion?

_____ 8. Are faculty provided with sufficient time to collaborate?

_____ 9. Does everybody know what they are supposed to do?

_____ 10. Do teams and pairs know how to work together?

_____ 11. Do the faculty know what to do in the classrooms?

_____ 12. Is an effective school-wide discipline plan in place?

_____ 13. Are faculty or parents particularly resistant to including students with certain types of disabilities?

_____ 14. Are the other students in the inclusive classroom prepared?

_____ 15. Do you have a monitoring plan?

© 2002 by PRO-ED, Inc.

CHAPTER FOUR

◆◆◆◆◆◆◆◆◆◆◆◆◆◆◆◆◆◆◆◆

What Are the Collaborative Teams in an Inclusive School?

◆ In this chapter a vision is shared of the various team structures in a collaborative and inclusive school. School professionals define collectively the specific team structures they plan to use in their collaborative and inclusive school. Some of these structures may already be in place within the school, some may be in place but need to be reconceptualized to reflect a more collaborative effort, and some may be new structures that will be implemented.

Following are four critical questions that school staff members should ask in determining which of the structures are best for them:

1. Do we have it?
2. Do we need it?
3. Do we need to eliminate it?
4. Do we need to improve it?

The school staff should apply each of the four questions to each of the organizational structures described below in order to realize their vision of a collaborative and inclusive school.

A Vision of a Collaborative and Inclusive School

Each school staff should create a concrete vision of a collaborative and inclusive school by first determining the various team structures that are being or could be used in order to facilitate effective schooling and cooperative group decision making. To encourage collaboration in the work environment, the group could then reach consensus on the expected professional behaviors (see Chapter 5).

The vision of collaboration should be reflected in the school-wide improvement plan. It is critical that school staff members, who are exploring the possibility of using collaboration in their schools, be able to envision the various ways in which the process of collaboration can be applied within the total school (Idol, 1996).

A collaborative and inclusive school can consist of six basic structures that have potential for building a sound base (see also Idol, 1996; Idol & West, 1991).

The structures include the following:

- a school-based management team;

- some committees of education professionals to make decisions regarding curricula, textbooks, testing efforts, instructional approaches, and so forth;

- both department- and grade-level instructional teams;

- some teacher assistance teams, which serve as prevention programs for students at risk for school failure;

- a collaborative teaching program, which requires coordination of special and general instructional planning and implementation and which provides both direct and indirect consultative services to support classroom instruction; and

- extended collaboration between school and community, comprised of both collaborative projects between school and community groups and interagency coordination and collaboration.

Following are more detailed descriptions of each of these team structures.

School-Based Management

In a collaborative and inclusive school, school-based management is used as an alternative to the more traditional practice of school district governance ordinarily carried out by centralized authority in the district office. On the contrary, with school-based management the school is the primary unit of educational decision making. The individuals responsible for implementing decisions are actually making those decisions, a concept endorsed by the American Association of School Administrators (AASA), the National Association of Elementary School Principals (NAESP), and the National Association of Secondary School Principals (NASSP) (AASA et al., 1988).

Two basic ideas underlie the use of school-based management. First, decisions are made at the level closest to the issue being addressed. Second, educational reform efforts will be more likely to be accomplished if those responsible for carrying out initiatives feel a sense of ownership and responsibility for the change effort.

School-based management can both empower and enable principals and teachers, as well as others in the community. School-based management teams are usually made up of the principal, who takes a major leadership role as the instructional leader of the school, and selected teachers, parents, and members of the community.

These members of the school-based management team have responsibility for making certain decisions about the budget, personnel, and curriculum (Kubick, 1988). For example, they might also be involved in developing new programs; developing scheduling to meet instructional objectives; allocating resources within the building; determining professional development needs; selecting supplemental instructional materials; and selecting applicants for positions within the school from a pool of prescreened candidates (as determined by the AASA/NAESP/NASSP taskforce).

Committees of Education Professionals

In a collaborative and inclusive school, committees of education professionals are needed to carry out certain tasks that require collaborative decision making and are designed to improve the school program. Such tasks might include selection of supplemental curricula, ascertaining that there is a match between the school and district curricula, determining appropriate matches between what is taught and what is tested, textbook selection at the district level, and so on. The committee tasks should be a part of the school's improvement plan.

Use of these professional committees allows members of the school faculty to be involved and empowered in various ways, and take leadership roles to set future directions. They also allow for more widespread faculty involvement than is represented in the school-based management team.

In collaborative and inclusive schools, these committees often serve as vehicles for staff development and growth, as well as for accomplishment of the specific tasks assigned to the committee. For example, in one elementary school a principal and a staff identified four areas for professional committee work, asking the faculty to assign themselves to a single committee for a year's duration. The committee areas for which solutions were to be determined collaboratively were ascertained with these questions: (a) How should instruction of thinking skills be embedded into the curriculum? (b) How should computerized instruction be incorporated in the classrooms? (c) How should reading and writing instruction be integrated? (d) What general improvements could be made in the school program? (The latter committee was formed for faculty who felt no commitment to any of the first three areas.)

These groups were then charged with studying the targeted problem area, searching various knowledge bases and resources, attending staff development sessions to determine plausible solutions, and reaching consensus on a final set of recommendations. An important distinction is that the recommendations formulated by the committee are actually implemented in the school. They are not simply offered as a possible solution to be considered. Thus, if faculty have strong opinions about particular areas of decision making, it behooves them to volunteer to work on the relevant professional committee.

It is sometimes laughingly said that the best way to kill a great idea is to assign the task of studying the idea to a committee. This common pitfall can be avoided if committees are expected to complete a plan of action that will be implemented and if they understand the distinction between cooperation and collaboration.

That is, many school staffs make efforts to cooperate, but probably far fewer are actually collaborating. In a synthesis of research on organizational collaboration, Hord (1986) made these important distinctions: In *cooperation*, two or more parties, each with separate and autonomous programs, agree to work together in making all such programs more successful; in *collaboration*, by contrast, the parties involved share responsibility and authority for basic policy decision making.

As these collaborative committees are formed, it is important to make clear the task of the committee. The task should include precise timelines for formulation of recommendations. The committee should be expected to produce a specified plan of action for carrying out the recommendations and impose a deadline for when the committee work will be completed. The plan of action should include delineation of subtasks, identification of responsible persons, and the setting of specific completion dates for each subtask.

Department and Grade-Level Instructional Teams

In collaborative and inclusive schools, it is expected that when faculty members join the staff, they are accepting shared responsibility for the learning and development of all students attending the school. A natural consequence of this philosophy is that teachers are expected to plan and teach in teams. In some schools, this collaboration occurs only for planning purposes; in other schools it occurs for both planning and instruction.

For example, in one elementary school, the principal and the faculty determined that grade-level instructional teams would be the primary means of providing support to teachers with students who were difficult to teach or at risk for school failure. This was an inner-city school where the majority of students was considered to be at risk (see Idol, 1994a). All grade-level teachers were required to be members of the grade-level instructional team, even though a small minority was reluctant to do so. Each grade-level team was required to meet once a week. Over a month's time, they were expected to spend about half their time working on instructional planning and coordination and the other half working on child-centered problems brought to the team by the individual team members. Relevant special and remedial education faculty members were involved in the latter on an as-needed basis.

Another example of this type of teaming can be found in most middle schools, where the Core Team concept is used. Core Teams are comprised of four academic subject teachers, two for math and science and two for language arts and social studies. These four teachers are responsible for all the students assigned to their core, usually about 100 students. Again, relevant special and remedial education faculty members are involved on an as-needed basis.

A third example is use of departmental teaming at the high school level. The high school program described in Chapter 1 is a good example of how departmental teams can be used for (a) strengthening the academic curriculum and for improving the quality of instruction, (b) making adaptations for students who are at risk for school failure, and (c) supporting one other in classroom management and student discipline projects.

Recall that in the example described in Chapter 1, each departmental chairperson was responsible for providing staff development on instructional adaptations to the departmental faculty. Faculty members were encouraged to work in teams as they explored various instructional adaptations. Faculty members were then expected to select certain adaptations, implement them, and report progress to the department chairperson.

Teacher Assistance Teams

Collaborative and inclusive schools with effective teacher assistance teams use a prevention-focused assistance system in which teachers request problem-solving time with a team of peers in order to explore solutions to unresolved classroom-related problems. In a collaborative and inclusive school, the team works together—with the teacher as a team member—to solve the problem, rather than simply offering an array of potential solutions to the teacher requesting assistance.

These teams always have some type of support staff—either special education teacher, guidance counselor, school psychologist, social worker, speech and language clinician, and so forth, often with more than one of these specialists. As an example, one elementary school in Wisconsin used this approach to significantly reduce referrals to special education and to maintain more students who were experiencing classroom-related problems in the general education program (Saver & Downes, 1990).

Many collaborative and inclusive schools utilize the concept of teacher assistance teams as a means of preventing certain students who are at risk for school failure from dropping out of school or from being referred to special education. As described by Chalfant and Van Dusen Pysh (1989):

> The teacher assistance team is a school-based, problem-solving unit used to assist teachers in generating strategies. A team usually consists of a core of three elected faculty members representing various grade levels or disciplines who assist other teachers. The classroom teacher requesting assistance serves as a fourth and equal member of the team. Team membership may vary by building and specific teacher need. Some teams, for example, include principals, special education personnel, and parents. (p. 50)

Although Chalfant and Van Dusen Pysh conceptualized the teacher assistance team as a vehicle to offer possible solutions to teachers, my colleagues and I have made one significant modification. In schools we have worked with, the team works together to solve the problem, rather than simply offering an array of potential solutions to the teacher requesting assistance.

We have trained school-based teams to use the collaborative problem-solving process in the following way: The teacher requests assistance from the team regarding the problem. The teacher requesting assistance joins the team and the team uses a six-step problem-solving process, which has evolved out of the school consultation literature, to not only identify the problem but to reach consensus on a plausible plan of action for solving the problem. These steps are described in detail in Chapter 5 (see also Idol, Paolucci-Whitcomb, & Nevin, 1986; West & Idol, 1990; West, Idol, & Cannon, 1989).

Collaborative Teaching Programs

The collaborative teaching program can include supporting classroom teachers in as many as four different ways: consulting teacher services, cooperative teaching in the classroom, supportive resource programs, and instructional assistants. Each of these services is delivered by staff working together collaboratively and each is viewed as an important means of supporting classroom teachers. In particular, collaboration leads to a reconceptualization of how special support programs can best be offered by both general and special education. Following are brief explanations of each of these student support structures.

Consulting Teacher Services

The consulting teacher model is a form of indirect special education service delivery where a certificated special education teacher serves as a consultant to a classroom teacher. Special education students receiving indirect services are taught by the classroom teacher. The consultant works indirectly with the targeted students by working

TABLE 4.1
Sample Role Description for a Consulting Teacher

Consulting teachers work indirectly with classroom teachers as a means of facilitating the progress of special education students who are included in the general education program or who are mainstreamed for part of the school day. Special education consultation is a process for providing special education services to students with special needs who are enrolled in general education. Consultation is (a) indirect, in that the special education consultant does not provide the instructional service to the student(s), (b) collaborative, in that all individuals involved in the consultative process are assumed to have expertise to contribute and responsibility to share for instructional outcomes, (c) voluntary, in that all parties are willing participants in the consultative process, and (d) problem-solving-oriented, in that the goal of consultation is to prevent or resolve student problems.

The types of services provided by the consulting teacher include the following:

1. collaborative involvement in the development of all IEPs for students receiving consulting teacher services;

2. monitoring of all IEPs for students receiving consulting teacher services;

3. provision of consultation services to classroom teachers;

4. help in solving student-related problems pertaining to academic problems, study skill problems, and behavior and discipline problems;

5. help in solving classroom-related problems pertaining to curricular modifications, instructional adaptations, and teaching arrangements;

6. help in facilitating successful transitions of students with disabilities who were previously in more restrictive special education placements and are now enrolled in either inclusive or mainstream classrooms;

7. provision of demonstration teaching and modeling of newly developed teaching innovations;

8. participation in collaborative problem solving with classroom teachers of inclusive or mainstream classrooms;

9. facilitation of involvement of parents of special education students to accommodate parental involvement in program development;

10. provision of classroom-based assessments using curriculum-based assessments, portfolio assessments, and classroom observations;

11. monitoring of student progress of all special education students assigned to consulting teacher services.

Note. Adapted from Idol (1989, 1993).

directly with the classroom teacher. The original Collaborative Consultation Model (Idol et al., 1986) was designed for use with consulting teacher services. A sample of a job description for a special education consulting teacher can be found in Table 4.1.

A slightly different version of the consulting teacher model is the resource/consulting teacher model (see Idol, 1989, 1993). This model forms a bridge between the resource teacher model and the consulting teacher model. Resource/consulting teachers provide special education services partially through the direct and partially through the indirect approach.

TABLE 4.2

Cooperative Teachers' Duties in Inclusive Classrooms

1. Monitor all IEPs for all identified special education students.

2. Check weekly progress for all identified special education students.

3. Meet with each grade level team once a week during the conference period or grade level meeting.

4. Preview classroom teachers' lesson plans, which are returned by Friday for the following week.

5. Monitor students who have instructional or curricular modifications.

6. Develop modified assignments and tests for students with special needs.

7. Work with classroom teachers to conduct portfolio assessments.

8. Develop behavior contracts for students with behavior problems.

9. Teach individual or small groups of students in the classroom.

10. Visit with students who need monitoring on an as-needed basis (e.g., "Do you have your homework? notebook? assignment sheet?" etc.).

11. Provide reteaching opportunities for certain students.

12. Support teachers with testing of individuals and groups.

Note. This job description was developed collaboratively by the faculty and staff at Lillian Elementary School in Alvarado School District, Alvarado, Texas, under the principalship of Karen Sero. Reprinted with permission.

Cooperative Teaching in the Classroom

Cooperative teaching (or co-teaching) refers to an educational approach in which general and special educators work in a co-active and coordinated fashion to teach jointly heterogeneous groups of students (academically and behaviorally) in educationally integrated settings (i.e., general classrooms) (Bauwens, Hourcade, & Friend, 1989, p. 18). These authors describe cooperative teaching as a direct and complementary outgrowth of the Collaborative Consultation Model (Idol et al., 1986). In the cooperative teaching model, special education and classroom teachers work together in the same classroom to provide educational programs for all students assigned to the classroom. For example, cooperative teaching was used in the elementary school described in Chapter 1. Table 4.2 lists the roles and responsibilities that faculty generated for the cooperating teacher in their building. There are several different arrangements that teachers engage in when cooperative teaching. Five of them are described in Table 4.3. Appendix 4.A is a co-teaching worksheet that can aid cooperative teachers in defining their strengths, challenges, and goals to be accomplished with cooperative teaching.

Supportive Resource Programs

Wiederholt and Chamberlain (1989) defined the resource room approach as follows:

The resource room is any setting in the school to which students come to receive specific instruction on a regularly scheduled basis, while receiving the majority of their

TABLE 4.3

Types of Co-Teaching Arrangements

Arrangement	Characteristics of Arrangement
One teacher–one support	• Lead teacher • Support teacher • Teachers do little cooperative planning
Station teaching	• Teachers divide the instructional content • Teachers share the content but have separate teaching responsibilities for various parts of the content
Parallel teaching	• Teachers both teach the same content • Teachers each deliver the content to one-half of the class • Teachers plan together
Alternative teaching	• One teacher teaches to one large group while one teacher teaches to a smaller group • In the smaller group, there is preteaching, reinforcement of previously taught content, and/or follow-up reteaching of large group content • Teachers plan together
Team teaching	• Teachers share instruction by teaching the large group together • There are coordinated activities within a single lesson • There is mutual trust and commitment between the cooperative teachers • Teachers plan together

Note. From *Cooperative Teaching: Rebuilding the Schoolhouse for all Students,* by J. Bauwens and J. J. Hourcade, 1995, Austin, TX: PRO-ED. Copyright 1994 by PRO-ED. Reprinted with permission.

education elsewhere (usually in a general school program). Therefore, resource rooms are not part-time special education classes where students with handicaps are integrated with peers only for lunch, gym, or art. They also are not consultative programs where students remain full-time in a general classroom setting and where modifications are made in instruction. Neither are they study halls, discipline or detention centers, or crisis rooms. (p. 15)

Supportive resource programs are those resource room programs that truly support the instruction and curriculum offered in the general classroom program. In supportive programs, resource teachers and classroom teachers collaborate in designing the contents of a student's individualized program of instruction for the resource room. The purpose of the collaboration is to ensure that the resource room program truly supports the general education program and is one that is likely to support students' transferring what they have learned in the resource room to learning in the general classroom.

Instructional Assistants

A third type of direct service option is to provide instructional assistants (paraprofessional aides) to inclusive classrooms. Typically, this is one of the first options school staffs choose for providing assistance to classroom teachers, particularly if they have not had preliminary preparation in building collaborative and inclusive schools. Often, such assistants are funded exclusively with special education monies to provide assistance to a single student with special education needs. The assistant then remains with that student throughout the school day. Using instructional assistants in this way is not, in my opinion, the best way to use this very important resource.

Instead, some school staffs have been experimenting with cross-funding instructional assistants, so they are partially funded from a combination of various funding sources, such as from monies for special education, remedial, bilingual, and general education funds. The assistants are assigned to classroom teachers and are available to help with any student who needs assistance, not just the special education student who is included. For example, in one school (see the elementary school example in Chapter 1 and refer to Idol, 1997a), this approach resulted in an instructional assistant for every two classroom teachers. In this school, the faculty worked as a team to define and determine exactly what they wanted the instructional assistants to do. Table 4.4 contains a list of the responsibilities assigned to the instructional assistants in that school.

Collaboration Between School and Community

There is another important aspect of collaboration that is important to this vision: collaboration between school and community. In the collaborative and inclusive school, interagency collaboration occurs for students with complex educational and rehabilitation needs. Members of these groups also form the interdisciplinary teams responsible for developing the Individualized Education Program (IEP).

TABLE 4.4
Instructional Assistants' Duties in Inclusive Classrooms

1. Work with students in small groups or 1:1.
2. Assist with modifications for students (highlighting text, oral reading, oral testing, etc.).
3. Assist with monitoring students and classroom observations.
4. Assist with reteaching students on specific skills.
5. Assist with portfolio assessments.
6. Assist with recording reading logs, assignment sheets, etc.
7. Listen to individual students read aloud.
8. Assist students during "Be an Author."
9. Assist with individual and small group testing.
10. Assist and supervise students during center time.
11. Assist in monitoring student progress.
12. Assist with keeping students on task.
13. Assist with monitoring student behavior/discipline management plan.
14. Provide special 1:1 assistance to students with disabilities.
15. Assist teacher during large-group discussion and presentations.
16. Assist in the making of instructional games.
17. Assist in classroom organization.
18. Assist in clerical duties during conference period or before and after school, as needed.

Note. This job description was developed collaboratively by the faculty and staff at Lillian Elementary School in Alvarado School District, Alvarado, Texas, under the principalship of Karen Sero. Reprinted with permission.

Interagency collaboration also occurs for various programs supporting students at risk for school failure and their families. For example, a secondary school might sponsor an effort to coordinate support programs for pregnant teenagers, with collaboration within the school program itself; a birth control program sponsored through a local hospital; a prenatal program sponsored through the same hospital; or a federally-sponsored community project for low-income families needing winter care and home heating assistance. Another example might be collaboration between the school and a center for family resource and youth services in order to coordinate and provide after-school day care for families with working parents and families in financial need.

Community and school collaboration also occurs in the development of new prevention programs for students at risk in life-sustaining areas. For example, a team of persons comprised of a high school counselor, a community health professional, a local clergy person, and two parents, developed an AIDS (acquired immuno deficiency syndrome) prevention program targeted for 11th and 12th graders in a community high school.

Another example of community and school collaboration concerns a group addressing a sex education program for sixth- and seventh-grade students in a middle school. The team was comprised of a sixth-grade counselor, a seventh-grade counselor, a psychologist who specializes in family relations and sex education, a parent of a middle-school child, a seventh-grade health science teacher, and a school nurse. This team had responsibility for previewing five commercially available sex education programs and the currently-adopted health science textbooks. They developed an instructional plan for using the current textbook, supplemented with select materials from the various sex education programs.

Summary

Thus, the collaborative and inclusive school consists of many different components, all requiring adults to work collaboratively. Some of that collaboration involves decision making and planning, some involves problem identification and problem solving, and some involves program implementation and evaluation. In particular, the special support programs in collaborative and inclusive schools are each influenced by the Collaborative Consultation Model, especially those that provide indirect service to classroom teachers.

In each of these various groups, all members are prepared to work collaboratively, including those centered within the school, those designed specifically to interface programs between general and special education, those involving interagency collaboration, and those involving school/community collaboration. All members use the collaborative decision-making process and have participated in adult development programs working on interactive, communication, problem-solving, and decision-making skills that are essential to the collaborative process (refer to Chapter 5 for a description of the staff development process). The primary point is that all of these structures require adults to interact and solve problems together. All are structures to which a collaborative decision-making process can be applied. And, all are structures that, when offered in concert, build a strong base for a collaborative work effort and a collaborative and inclusive school.

APPENDIX 4.A
Co-Teaching Worksheet

1. List the strengths you each bring to the co-teaching arrangement.

Classroom Teacher

_____

_____

_____

Special Education Teacher

_____

_____

_____

2. List the challenges you each bring to the co-teaching arrangement.

Classroom Teacher

_____

_____

_____

Special Education Teacher

_____

_____

_____

3. Place a star by the one challenge you both believe will be the most difficult to overcome.

4. Write a goal for how you both plan to overcome this challenge. In other words, what outcome do you hope to achieve by the end of this semester/year?

_____

_____

_____

5. *How* and *when* will you evaluate whether you have met this goal?

_____

_____

_____

Note: From *Co-Teaching Worksheet*, by L. Dieker, 1996, presented at Cooperative Teaching Training Seminar, Summer Institute for Creating Collaborative and Inclusion Schools, Lake Geneva, WI. Copyright 1996 by L. Dieker. Reprinted with permission.

CHAPTER FIVE

◆ ◆ ◆ ◆ ◆ ◆ ◆ ◆ ◆ ◆ ◆ ◆ ◆ ◆ ◆ ◆ ◆ ◆

How Do Faculty Become Collaborative Teams?

◆ This chapter is an explanation of how to develop collaborative teams among school faculty. Emphasis is placed on three areas: (1) the content of training needed for effective collaboration; (2) the process of how to prepare adults to work as collaborative team members within the various team structures (described in Chapter 4); and (3) guidance on how to evaluate both the team process and team productivity. The key concept is that in order for truly effective collaboration to occur, classroom teachers and support staff must be supported in learning how to collaborate. This support can take various forms, as discussed in this chapter.

Establishing a Collaborative Work Environment

In working to build a collaborative work environment, Roy and O'Brien (1989) proposed several norms for staff behavior that center around staff working together, giving one another feedback, and placing emphasis on making instruction the major priority. Appendix 2.A in Chapter 2 is an instrument for determining the degree of collaboration in the working environment of your school.

Creating a collaborative school is not a matter of merely installing new programs like peer coaching, collaborative teaching, or a teacher assistance team. Rather, it has to do with building and sustaining a new culture within the school environment in which professional behaviors like those listed in Table 5.1 become the norm rather than the exception.

This questionnaire (see Appendix 2.A) is used in a faculty meeting as an initial activity to support a school staff in their examination of how collaborative they think their group actually is. It is recommended that members of the staff each respond to these 10 questions and compare reactions in small discussion groups.

Reactions are then shared with the entire group so that the group at large (a) clarifies what the consensual opinion of the group is and (b) selects certain items from the questionnaire as target areas that need improvement or emphasis. These items are then included in the School-Wide Improvement Plan with specific activities or approaches that would be implemented and specified timelines for their completion.

TABLE 5.1
Essential Skills for the Process of Consultation

Consultation Theory/Models

1. Practice reciprocity of roles between consultant and consultee in facilitating the consultation process.

2. Demonstrate knowledge of various stages/phases of the consultation process.

3. Assume joint responsibility for identifying each stage of the consultation process and adjusting behavior accordingly.

4. Match consultation approach(es) to specific consultation situation(s), setting(s) and need(s).

Research on Consultation Theory Training and Practice

5. Translate relevant consultation research findings into effective school-based consultation practice.

Personal Characteristics

6. Exhibit ability to be caring, respectful, empathic, congruent, and open in consultation interactions.

7. Establish and maintain rapport with all persons involved in the consultation process, in both formal and informal interactions.

8. Identify and implement appropriate responses to stage of professional development of all persons involved in the consultation process.

9. Maintain positive self-concept and enthusiastic attitude throughout the consultation process.

10. Demonstrate willingness to learn from others throughout the consultation process.

11. Facilitate progress in consultation situations by managing personal stress, maintaining calm in time of crisis, taking risks, and remaining flexible and resilient.

12. Respect divergent points of view, acknowledging the right to hold different views and to act in accordance with convictions.

Interactive Communication

13. Communicate clearly and effectively in oral and written form.

14. Utilize active ongoing listening and responding skills to facilitate the consultation process (e.g., acknowledging, paraphrasing, reflecting, clarifying, elaborating, summarizing).

15. Determine own and others' willingness to enter the consultative relationship.

16. Adjust consultation approach to the learning stage of individuals involved in the consultation process.

17. Exhibit ability to grasp and validate overt/covert meaning and affect in communications (perceptive).

18. Interpret nonverbal communications of self and others (e.g., eye contact, body language, personal boundaries in space) in appropriate context.

(*continues*)

TABLE 5.1 *Continued.*

Interactive Communication

19. Interview effectively to elicit information, share information, explore problems, set goals and objectives.

20. Pursue issues with appropriate persistence once they arise in consultation process.

21. Give and solicit continuous feedback that is specific, immediate, and objective.

22. Give credit to others for their ideas and accomplishments.

23. Manage conflict and confrontation skillfully throughout the consultation process to maintain collaborative relationships.

24. Manage timing of consultation activities to facilitate mutual decision making at each stage of the consultation process.

25. Apply the principles of positive reinforcement to one another in the collaborative team situation.

26. Be willing and safe enough to say, "I don't know … let's find out."

Collaborative Problem Solving

27. Recognize that successful and lasting solutions require commonality of goals and collaboration throughout all phases of the problem-solving process.

28. Develop a variety of data collection techniques for problem identification and clarification.

29. Generate viable alternatives through brainstorming techniques characterized by active listening, nonjudgmental responding, and appropriate reframing.

30. Evaluate alternatives to anticipate possible consequences, narrow and combine choices, and assign priorities.

31. Integrate solutions into a flexible, feasible, and easily implemented plan of action relevant to all persons affected by the problem.

32. Adopt a "pilot problem-solving" attitude, recognizing that adjustments to the plan of action are to be expected.

33. Remain available throughout implementation for support, modeling, and/or assistance in modification.

34. Redesign, maintain, or discontinue interventions using data-based evaluation.

35. Utilize observation, feedback, and interviewing skills to increase objectivity and mutuality throughout the problem-solving process.

Systems Change

36. Develop role as a change agent (e.g., implementing strategies for gaining support, overcoming resistance).

37. Identify benefits and negative effects that could result from change efforts.

(continues)

TABLE 5.1 *Continued.*

Equity Issues and Values/Beliefs Systems

38. Facilitate equal learning opportunities by showing respect for individual differences in physical appearance, race, sex, handicap, ethnicity, religion, SES, or ability.

39. Advocate for services that accommodate the educational, social, and vocational needs of all students, with or without special education problems

40. Encourage implementation of laws and regulations designed to provide appropriate education for all students with handicapping conditions.

41. Utilize principles of the least restrictive environment in all decisions regarding students with handicapping conditions.

42. Modify myths, beliefs, and attitudes that impede successful social and educational integration of handicapped students into the least restrictive environment.

43. Recognize, respect, and respond appropriately to the effects of personal values and belief systems of self and others in the consultation process.

Evaluation of Consultation Effectiveness

44. Insure that persons involved in planning and implementing the consultation process are also involved in its evaluation.

45. Establish criteria for evaluating input, process, and outcome variables affected by the consultation process.

46. Engage in self-evaluation of strengths and weaknesses to modify personal behaviors influencing the consultation process.

47. Utilize continuous evaluative feedback to maintain, revise, or terminate consultation activities.

Note. From *Collaboration in the Schools: Interacting, Communicating, and Problem Solving,* by J. F. West, L. Idol, and G. Cannon, 1989, Austin, TX: PRO-ED. Copyright 1988 by PRO-ED. Reprinted with permission.

Preparing Teams To Collaborate

One of the biggest mistakes educators make in trying to build a more collaborative school is expecting that school staff can simply decide to be more collaborative. People need to be prepared to collaborate by being provided with specific training experiences, including specific team practices to use; appropriate use of interpersonal and interactive communication skills; group decision-making skills, including the art of negotiation and consensus building; and a specific method for resolution of problems.

The Interactive and Communicative Process Skills

Collaborators need to be prepared to competently use a number of communicative and interactive skills integral to the group problem-solving process. The first stage in preparing teams to collaborate is to conduct a needs assessment of team members' current levels of expertise in team process skills.

West and Cannon (1988) identified and validated 47 different essential collaborative consultation competencies needed by both classroom teachers and special educators, working together to develop collaborative instructional programs for students with special needs. These skills are listed in Table 5.1.

These 47 skills have been developed into a staff development program for teachers, support staff, and administrators that offers preparatory and practice opportunities on each of the skills (see West, Idol, & Cannon, 1989). There is a guided training module for each of the 47 skills. This program is also used for preservice education in school collaboration.

Seven of these skills center on the personal characteristics that effective consultants bring to the collaborative process. Fourteen are essential interactive communication skills, and 11 specifically address collaborative problem solving. For optimal benefit, it is recommended that the program be used in concert with this book.

Group Decision Making

With the Collaborative Consultation Model (see Chapter 2) teams practice reciprocity of involvement, the team structure is parity-based, and consensus is reached in each stage before progressing to the subsequent stage. Team members engage in this six-stage process to solve problems related to student learning and behavior; student management; curriculum; instruction; student support; and so forth. These are the most commonly accepted stages in the interdisciplinary school consultation literature, and are described by Idol, Nevin, & Paolucci-Whitcomb (1994) as follows:

◆ Stage 1: Goal/Entry

During this stage, roles, objectives, responsibilities and expectations of all team members are negotiated. Formal or informal contracts may be developed to reflect the agreements. (Note that this is not the goal setting for the student, but rather for the team itself; the latter occurs during the Intervention Recommendations stage.) Also, during this first stage, team members set two other types of goals: team process goals and intrapersonal goals. These are discussed in more detail later in this chapter.

◆ Stage 2: Problem Identification

During this stage the nature and parameters of the identified problem are clearly defined, so all members of the team have a mutual understanding of the problem. Once the problem has been identified clearly, the team sets a goal reflecting how the problem behavior(s) will look when it has been corrected.

◆ Stage 3: Intervention Recommendations

During this stage potential interventions are generated and the effects of each are predicted. Recommendations are prioritized in the order in which they will be implemented and the final recommendation is selected. Written, measurable objectives are developed to (a) specify intervention details for each aspect of the problem, (b) identify criteria for determining if the problem has been solved, and (c) delineate activities and procedures for all involved and identify resources needed to implement intervention strategies.

◆ Stage 4: Implementation Recommendations

During this stage implementation occurs according to the established objectives and procedures. Here, each stage in implementing the intervention selected is specified, along with timelines for completion and identification of responsible personnel. Responsibility for actual implementation, as determined in the previous stage, may rest entirely with the classroom teacher or with a combination of team members. However, the entire team has mutual and ultimate responsibility for the success or failure of the intervention plan.

◆ Stage 5: Evaluation

During this stage the success of the intervention strategies designed to solve problems is evaluated. Evaluation of the intended program includes measurement of (a) student progress, (b) changes in adult team members' knowledge, skills, attitudes, and behaviors, and (c) changes in the school system or overall program.

◆ Stage 6: Redesign

During this stage the intervention is continued, redesigned, or discontinued on the basis of team evaluation of the intervention strategies.

Following is a basic set of collaborative skills that are represented by particular modules from the *Collaboration in the School* staff development curriculum (West et al., 1989):

1. Demonstrate knowledge of various stages/phases of the consultation process (Module 2).

2. Demonstrate tacit knowledge of four basic models of consultation (Module 2) and mastery of the collaborative model.

3. Use active, ongoing listening and responding skills to facilitate the collaborative consultation process (e.g., acknowledging, paraphrasing, reflecting, clarifying, elaborating, and summarizing) (Module 14).

4. Interview effectively to elicit information, share information, explore problems, set goals and objectives (Module 19).

5. Develop skills in systematic identification of problems (see Module 28; see also Chapter 5 in Idol et al., 1994).

6. Generate viable alternatives through brainstorming techniques characterized by active listening, nonjudgmental responding, and appropriate reframing (Module 29).

7. Evaluate intervention alternatives to anticipate possible consequences, narrow and combine choices, and assign priorities (Module 30).

8. Integrate solutions into a flexible, feasible, and easily implemented Action Plan relevant to all persons affected by the problem (Module 31).

Generic Principles of Collaborative Consultation

As collaborative teams use this problem-solving process, all team members are expected to adhere to and practice a set of generic principles of Collaborative Consultation.

These principles are listed in Table 2.2 in Chapter 2. Team members who apply these principles will likely find improvement in their attitudes toward other team members and toward the overall quality of team production.

The content of collaborative staff development described thus far includes determining how collaborative the current working environment is; establishing areas to improve for making a school more collaborative; and training teams in the interactive and communicative process skills, the six stages of collaborative problem solving, and understanding and application of the generic principles of Collaborative Consultation. Following is a description of the basic format used to prepare the teams in these areas.

Preparation of Collaborative Teams

Selection of Program Participants

A training effort such as this can be focused on interdisciplinary groups of professionals representing school administration, general education, school psychology, special education, guidance and counseling, speech and language services, and other related services. Paraprofessionals, parents, and older students are included on problem-solving teams when appropriate. One of our most successful efforts in helping to bring about change in schools has been to train building-based leadership teams. The purpose for building these teams is to develop a core of individuals that has been prepared in group decision making, collaborative team building, and effective communication and group interaction skills. This team then serves as a turn-around training team, offering similar training experiences to the entire school staff.

The first member of the team is the building principal, who is recruited on a voluntary basis. The principal either selects or the staff nominates key staff as leadership team members. In the beginning, a small core of classroom teachers is selected. These teachers should be influential among the school staff. These teachers may or may not be the most effective instructors in the building, but they are often those professionals to whom other teachers turn for guidance. Then, support staff are selected, such as resource and special program teachers who are responsible for auxiliary instruction for particular at-risk, remedial, and/or special education students. Finally, other key support staff members, who would enhance the development of the leadership team, are selected. These persons usually include one or more of the following specialists, depending on the needs of the team: school psychologist, guidance counselor, speech/language clinician, social worker, and so on.

In addition to the initial leadership team, this type of collaborative training can be provided to all faculty and staff who will be working on any type of collaborative team. The types of collaborative teams are described in Chapter 4. An economical and feasible strategy is to use the leadership team to train the other adults serving on the various team structures.

Organization of the Staff Development Program Agenda

As described earlier, all adults involved in the training complete a needs assessment to determine other skills in personal characteristics, interactive communication, change agent, and equity issues and to evaluate value/belief systems that need improvement. Based on the needs assessment data, staff development program developers construct a tentative agenda containing training modules in areas that the majority of the staff have indicated as being high priority areas. In addition, the consultants and those staff responsible for staff development efforts examine the list of skill areas that have not been indicated as high priorities but are essential components to developing effective functioning teams. If there are any such items, then those skill areas are added to the training program.

Team Process Training

Teams are formed consisting of four to five people. Ordinarily, a number of teams are trained simultaneously. One option is to identify the team structures (see Chapter 4) that will be utilized in your school and then train team members for each of these teams simultaneously. A second option is to train a leadership team that will later train the members of the various other team structures to be used in your building. If this option is chosen, a number of leadership teams can be trained by cost-sharing with other buildings or school districts.

Rotating team member roles.   Once the teams to be trained are established, then the entire training sequence is covered with the team(s). Individual team member roles are assigned within each team, including: timekeeper, recorder, and team spokesperson. These roles are rotated across all team members so that each time a new team task is assigned, a different member takes the role.

It is important that timekeepers be assertive, reminding the team periodically of the time remaining for task completion. Recorders participate fully in the team decision-making process, as well as record the team decisions on the Collaborative Problem-Solving Worksheet (see Appendix 5.A). Team spokespeople are careful in reporting the work and decisions of the team to others by reporting the team's consensual decision or position, not the personal perspective of the reporting individual.

The generic principles of collaborative consultation.   Team members are then given the generic principles of Collaborative Consultation (see Table 2.1 in Chapter 2). The various principles are discussed, referring to the Collaborative Consultation textbook (Idol, Nevin, & Paolucci-Whitcomb, 1994) for further explanation of each principle.

Intrapersonal attitudes and beliefs.   In the Collaborative Consultation Model, the intrapersonal attitudes and beliefs toward inclusion and related collaborative efforts are integral ingredients. As with the principles of Collaborative Consultation, individual team members explore those attitudes and beliefs that lie within oneself, with an eye for finding those that might impede work toward building a more collaborative and inclusive school (see also Table 2.3 in Chapter 2).

Goals for the Team

Intrapersonal goals.   At the beginning of the problem-solving process, Stage 1: Goal/ Entry, each team member selects certain principles of Collaborative Consultation or intrapersonal attitudes or beliefs or personal communication skills (see Table 5.1 and Chapter 9) they will be working on as they work with the team. During this stage, each member sets one or more intrapersonal goals for improving any of the principles or intrapersonal beliefs and attitudes or communication process skills discussed above.

Team process goals.   Also during the first stage, the team identifies one or more group process skills they want to improve on as a team. For example, these might be any of the communicative or group interaction skills listed in Table 5.1 under the categories of Personal Characteristics, Interactive Communication, or Collaborative Problem Solving.

Team production goals.   Also during the first stage, the team sets one or more team production goals. These goals center on system changes that the team foresees as area(s) likely to be impacted as a result of the team's solving the targeted problem. Examples of these can be found in Table 5.1 under the category of Systems Change.

Some other examples of types of systems variables influenced by collaborative teams might include reducing referrals to special education; increasing the number of students at risk for school failure; making positive changes in the classroom; selecting improved or adapted curricula; changing how teachers are teaching or working together; modifying the school-wide discipline plan; and so on. All of these examples reflect how the work of the team might result in a broader and more generalized application of what team members have taught one another as a result of working together. This truly is the ultimate goal of collaborative teamwork.

The Team Problem-Solving Process

The primary base of training lies in learning to use the six-stage problem-solving process described earlier in this chapter. Relying on the *Collaboration in the Schools* staff development program (particularly Modules 29, 30, & 31), collaborators learn to execute this process.

Emphasis is placed on establishing reciprocity and parity among the team members. *Reciprocity* means that all team members "have equal access to information and the opportunity to participate in problem identification, discussion, decision making and all final outcomes" (West et al., 1989, p. 4). *Parity* means that all team members are viewed as being of equal status in the collaborative team, regardless of gender, race, education, experience, age, occupation, and so on. Parity is applied even if the team members include a student, a parent, a paraprofessional assistant, and so on.

Reaching consensus.   Team members are taught a consensus-building process via the six stages in the problem-solving process. They apply six simple rules for reaching consensus (see Table 5.2). Reaching consensus is defined as achieving an agreement that every member of the team can live with morally and professionally. Reaching consensus does not mean that an individual team member will have everything turn out exactly as they had wanted, but rather results in solutions that all members of the team can support with integrity.

Completing the team decision-making process.   During training each team works through the six stages of the problem-solving process with a real problem they are currently facing. The instructor's manual in *Collaboration in the Schools* (see West et al., 1989) is used to teach each of the six stages. A demonstration videotape (Idol & West, 1989)

TABLE 5.2

Group Consensus Rules

1. Avoid arguing for your own individual judgments.

2. Approach the task on the basis of logic.

3. Avoid changing your mind only in order to reach agreement and to avoid conflict.

4. Support only those solutions with which you are able to agree at least somewhat.

5. Avoid "conflicting-reducing" techniques such as majority voting, averaging, or trading in reaching decisions.

6. View differences of opinion as being helpful, rather than as a hindrance in decision making.

also is available that illustrates this six-stage process. The videotape shows a team comprised of two people, a classroom teacher and a resource/consulting teacher, working together to include a former special education student in a fifth grade classroom.

Expanding the training program. In addition, other training experiences are included, relying on the needs assessment to determine areas of priority for the teams to be trained. Typically, these include training in various communication skills (see Chapter 9); clarifications on what inclusion means (see Chapter 3); and skills in managing conflict and confrontation in a positive manner (see Chapter 10). The content of a suggested staff development program is elaborated upon in Chapter 10.

First, it is important to establish the collaborative teams and train them in the collaborative process. Second, it is important to determine that the teams, based on evaluative feedback, are functioning well. Third, a more in-depth exploration of techniques for including students with challenges in general classes can be explored via staff development opportunities. This particular order is recommended because if teams are not functioning well, implementation of a sound inclusion program does not typically happen, even if individual team members possess great knowledge in how to do so. Also, I have found that teams have much material and experience to draw upon for teaching one another about how to implement inclusion programs in the classroom. Most teachers possess a great and diverse knowledge base. Creating a viable mechanism via the team structure is the means by which these team members can teach each other.

If teams determine they want more staff development in how to create and implement inclusion programs, there is a broad array of topics that can be explored. Some of the basic topics can be found in Idol and West's (1993) staff development program on effective instruction of difficult-to-teach students (see also Chapters 6, 7, and 8 in this book and Chapters 6 and 7 in Idol et al., 1994, as well as Bauwens & Hourcade, 1995; Lovitt, 1991; Meltzer et al., 1996; and Thousand, Villa, & Nevin, 1994).

Evaluating the Team Process

Periodically, the team takes the time to evaluate the team process. It is recommended this be done in three ways: *informally*, as a group during the team meetings; *personally*, by individual team members; and *formally*, as a group every 4 to 6 weeks.

Informal Team Evaluation

As teams are working together they stop occasionally and evaluate how their team process is progressing. Table 5.3 contains 10 questions the team uses to examine whether they are really reaching consensus in their decisions. This form can be used efficiently by having one person read the questions and having all team members look at one another and use their nonverbal skills to react to how well the team is progressing. This method also provides the team an opportunity to practice reading nonverbal messages, which is an integral part of the consensus-building process. Humans often send stronger messages with nonverbal cues (i.e., with face, eyes, mouth, body posture, etc.) than they do with their voices. Group discussion follows this nonverbal process.

Individual Team Member Evaluation

Individual team members occasionally examine their own personal progress in collaborative teamwork. There are two suggested ways to do this. One is to go over the principles of collaborative consultation (see Table 2.1), asking oneself whether those principles are being practiced. Another is to reexamine one's progress toward the intrapersonal goal(s) set during Stage 1 of the problem-solving process.

Formal Team Evaluation

About every four to six weeks, the entire team stops and formally evaluates their progress. Appendix 5.B contains 20 questions the team uses as a means of group examination. The outcomes of this evaluation form the basis for setting new team process goals as the previously set ones are mastered.

Summary

This chapter has been an examination of the process used by an effective collaborative team. A detailed summary of the content of appropriate preparatory experiences for such a team has been presented. This content has then been applied to a suggested sequence of training activities and practices, which many educators in several countries have used to build more collaborative schools. Finally, simple methods for evaluating the progress of a collaborative team have been explored.

TABLE 5.3
Evaluation of Group Consensus

1. Did the group really go by consensus? Or, did we gloss over conflicts?
2. Did the group stay on the intellectual or task aspects?
3. Did we stop to examine our process to see how we could work more effectively?
4. How satisfied are you with the way the group worked?
5. How efficient was the group?
6. How satisfied are you (as members) with the group?
7. How much influence did you feel you had as an individual on the group decision?
8. Did the group listen to you? Ignore you?
9. Did you stay involved in the teamwork or did you give up?
10. In what ways could you change or improve your interaction with others?

APPENDIX 5.A
Collaborative Problem-Solving Worksheet

Date _____

Team Members _____

_____

STEP 1: Problem Identification

What is the problem?

_____

_____

STEP 2: Problem Clarification

Hypothesis Generation:
What are some possible reasons for this problem?

1. _____

2. _____

3. _____

4. _____

5. _____

6. _____

7. _____

8. _____

Information Gathering:
Turn the hypothesis into a question by asking "What do we need?" OR "How could this be different?" OR "Who could do this?" OR "Is it helpful to determine this?" OR "What would we do so we can find out how valid the problem is?" OR "Is it relevant?"

1. _____

2. _____

3. _____

© 2002 by PRO-ED, Inc.

Analysis/Synthesis:
How has your understanding of the problem been clarified?

_____

_____

_____

_____

What is the most likely reason for the problem?

_____

_____

_____

_____

STEP 3: Development of a Plan

What could you do to solve the problem? Identify a number of possible solutions. Then pick one possible solution that would be best to try first.

Possible Solutions	Pros	Cons	Prioritize
1. _____	_____	_____	_____
2. _____	_____	_____	_____
3. _____	_____	_____	_____
4. _____	_____	_____	_____
5. _____	_____	_____	_____
6. _____	_____	_____	_____
7. _____	_____	_____	_____

Solution To Be Tried First

_____

_____

_____

© 2002 by PRO-ED, Inc.

STEP 4: Implementation of the Plan

What is necessary to carry out the plan? Formulate a timeline. Develop your Action Plan to implement the solution to be tried first.

Action Plan:

Implementation Steps	By Whom?	By When?
_____	_____	_____
_____	_____	_____
_____	_____	_____
_____	_____	_____

How will the plan be monitored?

_____

_____

STEP 5: Evaluation/Follow-Up

How will progress be evaluated?

_____

_____

Was the plan implemented? Did it work? If it did, great! If not, use this as new information in recycling the problem-solving process.

_____

_____

_____

Date and Time of Next Meeting

_____

Comments

_____

_____

_____

Note. Adapted from Idol (1997) and West, Idol, & Cannon (1989).

© 2002 by PRO-ED, Inc.

APPENDIX 5.B
Worksheet for Evaluating the Team Process

Directions: Use the following scale to determine your team's progress on how well you are working together.

1 = We have mastered this one and practice it regularly
2 = We are working on this one, but still don't use it consistently
3 = We know we need this one, but we are not using it
4 = We do not think we need this one

_____ 1. The team meets at a regularly scheduled time that is convenient for all.

_____ 2. Supportive teaching assistance is provided so team members can meet.

_____ 3. Our meetings are efficiently run as we use our time well.

_____ 4. We complete our agenda items in the expected amount of time.

_____ 5. We enjoy our work together.

_____ 6. We use a problem-solving worksheet to facilitate our team process.

_____ 7. Our team views our projects as collaborative with all team members feeling responsibility for success.

_____ 8. We view differences of opinion as one of our team strengths.

_____ 9. We use appropriate listening and responding skills.

_____ 10. We treat one another with respect.

_____ 11. Ours is an equality-based team, practicing parity and reciprocity.

_____ 12. We are skilled in clarifying problems and articulating problem statements.

_____ 13. Our goals are achievable, based on our recent history.

_____ 14. We are efficient at discerning which of a variety of problem solutions are the better ones.

_____ 15. We deal with conflict and confrontation openly and appropriately.

_____ 16. We use simple and effective methods of evaluating progress toward solving the problem.

_____ 17. We use simple and effective methods of evaluating our team process.

_____ 18. If a project does not turn out well, we come back together for a redesign meeting to work on more problem solving.

_____ 19. We keep a record of our projects via the problem-solving worksheets.

_____ 20. We celebrate our accomplishments.

© 2002 by PRO-ED, Inc.

◆◆◆◆◆◆◆◆◆◆◆◆◆◆◆◆◆◆◆◆

CHAPTER SIX

Disruptive Students Are the Worst! How Can They Be Included?

◆ Teachers often have strong opinions about which types of students with challenges are easiest or most difficult to include in education programs. Sometimes they say students with learning disabilities or those who do not read well are the most challenging to include, because it's more difficult to make adaptations in instruction than it is to include students for social reasons. Sometimes they say it is the student with multiple challenges and a very low intelligence who is most difficult to include. Often, their opinions change over time as they glean more and more experience in including different types of students. However, nearly every time the more experienced teachers are asked, especially classroom teachers, they agree that students with disruptive behaviors are truly the most difficult to include.

Equal Expectations for All

Students who are disruptive not only keep themselves from learning; they prevent others from learning as well, and take up inordinate amounts of teacher time. In working with classroom teachers, I have found it important to establish a firm, two-part policy regarding inclusion of students who are disruptive. First, no student should be allowed in a general education classroom who is a danger to him- or herself, to the teacher, or to the other students in the class.

Second, special education students should be expected to adhere to the same behavior standards as any other student attending the school. Exceptions should not be made for special education students who have identified behavior disorders or emotional disturbance. The same rules and expectations for acceptable and civilized behavior should be required of all students. With special education students, it is likely that an adapted behavior management plan will be developed and included in the Individualized Education Program (IEP). However, the expectations for acceptable student behavior should remain constant. Exceptions should not be made. In my experience as a school consultant, I have found that once this two-part policy is established, classroom teachers appear more comfortable about inclusion and more amenable to talking about which students might be included and how to accomplish that effort.

Levels of Intensity of Intervention

As teams engage in decision making, they have found it beneficial to use the Levels of Intensity of Intervention for Effective Student Management (see Table 6.1). This is a decision-making tool for assisting teams of educators in determining the most educationally enhancing environment for students with challenging behavioral and emotional problems. This framework, developed by Idol and West (1993, p. 90), stems from their earlier work in developing similar decision-making frameworks for students with reading difficulties (Idol, Lloyd, & West, 1988); in adapting curriculum and instruction for students with special learning needs or who are at risk for failure in school (West, Idol, & Cannon, 1989); and in adapting curriculum (Idol & West, 1993, p. 91).

The levels provide a framework as a team searches for the most appropriate ways to help students take responsibility for their own behavior. The eight levels in this model are described in Table 6.1. It is important to note that the questions in the framework address how intensive the intervention should be (see earlier work by Fagen [1986]).

Typically, education professionals first ask where students should be educated when they receive special services. The specific program is developed to fit the physical

TABLE 6.1
Levels of Intensity of Intervention for Effective Student Management

Level 1	Which behaviors the student exhibits in the general classroom can be judged at the same performance standard as those of normally achieving students?
Level 2	Which desirable behaviors can be maintained in the general classroom, but with adjustments in performance acceptability or by stating explicitly the expected classroom behavior?
Level 3	Which appropriate student behaviors can be maintained in the general classroom by structuring the classroom conditions with a classroom management plan?
Level 4	Which appropriate student behaviors can be expected in the general classroom with minor adjustments in the classroom management plan, such as planned ignoring of undesirable behavior, teacher signaling of discriminative stimuli, or teacher modeling of expected classroom behaviors?
Level 5	Which appropriate student behaviors can be expected in the general classroom by restructuring the classroom environment in which the undesirable behaviors are occurring or by conferencing with the student?
Level 6	Which undesirable student behaviors could be eliminated by identifying incompatible desirable behaviors and providing positive reinforcement for desirable behaviors and/or warnings for occurrences of undesirable behaviors?
Level 7	Which undesirable student behaviors require explicit enforcement of consequences, regulated permission, contracting, or use of token systems?
Level 8	Which undesirable student behaviors are of such a serious nature that immediate crisis intervention is needed?

Note. From *Effective Instruction for Difficult-To-Teach Students*, by L. Idol and J. F. West, 1993, Austin, TX: PRO-ED. Copyright 1993 by PRO-ED. Reprinted with permission. (The information in this table was originally adapted from Fagan [1986], Glasser [1977], and Idol, West, and Lloyd [1988].)

location of the program—that is, in the general classroom, in a resource program, special education classroom, special or alternative school, treatment clinic or hospital, and so on.

In contrast, teams using the Levels of Intensity of Intervention framework ask *how* and *what* questions first. How can the student best be managed? What types of interventions seem to be the most appropriate? These questions are asked in order to find the most educationally enhancing environment for the student. Only after these questions are answered to the best abilities of the collaborating team is the *where* question answered by reviewing the types of available services and programs. In using this framework teams are encouraged to select the least intensive interventions and to search for the most normal learning environment possible.

In the development of this framework, it was necessary to use a considerable amount of behavioral terminology for describing various types of interventions. For this reason, the framework is accompanied by two sets of definitions of terms: one of techniques for reducing undesirable behaviors and one of techniques for increasing desirable behaviors. These definitions are embedded in the text of this chapter (see section on Various Types of Techniques for Inclusion of Troubled or Troubling Students).

Application in an Elementary School

The faculty in one elementary school (see Idol, 1994a) fine-tuned the framework, clarifying when to use which staff members for intervention with students who were troubled or troubling to others. Depending on the Level of Intensity, the adjustments were as follows:

Levels 1, 2, & 3:	The problems would be handled by the classroom teacher.
Levels 4, 5, & 6:	The problems would be referred by the classroom teacher to the grade level team, who would handle the problem.
Level 7:	The problems would be referred to and handled by the grade level team or referred to building-based support staff, such as consulting teacher, special education teacher, counselor, etc.
Level 8:	The problems would be referred to the administrative staff.

The adapted framework proved helpful in this school, which most would consider to be a high-risk school; it was a typical inner-city school in America. The enrollment was relatively high, with a little more than 900 students in two groups: A magnet school section of approximately 300 students, comprised of mixed races but predominantly European American, and a neighborhood section of approximately 600 students. The student enrollment in the neighborhood section was 90% African American, 8% Hispanic American, and 2% European American. (The fact that the school was de facto segregated caused problems for the teachers and students in the neighborhood section.)

The faculty represented all three racial groups and the distribution was fairly equitable. The principal was African American and had been the principal at this school for many years. She was one of the most respected principals in the district and was well respected in this school. Over 60% of the students in the neighborhood section qualified for Title I monies and over 90% for free meal programs (breakfast and lunch). Over 50% of the children had one or more parents who were incarcerated. It was most definitely a high-risk school with a dedicated teaching faculty and quality leadership. The neighborhood section was the one where the Levels of Intensity framework was used.

How To Know When To Include

When a collaborative team is faced with deciding whether to include a student with behavior or emotional problems in a general classroom, certain practices should be followed. First, as noted, the same standards for acceptable and civilized behavior are expected of all students. Second, the team uses the Levels of Intensity of Intervention to determine if the inclusion placement for a student is appropriate and if so, how intensive the intervention and level of support from special education staff should be.

Then, the team ensures that five conditions be guaranteed when including such students. Nicholas J. Long, noted and distinguished authority on the education of students with behavior and emotional problems (Long, 1994, pp. 22–23), identified the five conditions as follows:

1. The school staff must meet and agree to participate in the inclusion effort.

2. A student with emotional disturbance should not be assigned to a classroom teacher by an administrator. A mutual process between the administrator and the teacher should take place to find the best fit between the teacher and the student. The receiving classroom teacher also must be willing to serve as this student's advocate.

3. The support staff, including the principal, must agree to participate in advanced crisis intervention training in order to have the skills to support the classroom teacher and the student during times of conflict.

4. The classroom group must be open to accepting new students, or at least not scapegoat or reject them.

5. The student with emotional disturbance must function no more than 2 years below the academic norm of the classroom, be motivated to keep up with the daily academic assignments, use the support staff, and make a personal commitment to the placement.

A final condition to add would be that the parents or guardians of the students be members of the collaborative team, have participated in the development of the Individualized Education Program for the student, and fully support the conditions of the placement in the inclusive classroom. Once these practices and conditions have been put into place, the collaborative team determines exactly which way of supporting the student and the classroom teacher is most appropriate. In the section that follows, some techniques for including troubled and troubling students are described.

Various Techniques for Inclusion of Troubled or Troubling Students

These suggested techniques for intervening with troubled or troubling students are organized into two categories: one of techniques for increasing desirable behaviors and one of techniques for reducing undesirable behaviors. Each of these techniques is embedded within the Levels of Intensity of Intervention for Effective Student Management (see Table 6.1). For each a definition is given followed by two examples of application, one for elementary and one for secondary students in inclusive classrooms.

Increasing Desirable Behaviors

Stating expectations. Clearly establish classroom behavior expectations, preferably with student input and agreement.

Elementary example: In Mark's fifth grade class, his teacher had five simply stated behavior expectations: Listen to others, treat others with respect, have your tools ready for learning, be willing to help others, and use gentle words. These rules were posted on the classroom wall. Mark and his teacher met for 3 to 5 minutes twice a week and discussed examples of these rules and how Mark was progressing with them. He concentrated on improving his responses to one rule at a time. He and the teacher then added a new rule when a previously targeted one was mastered.

Secondary example: In this 10th grade English class, students were expected to turn in written chapter summaries every three days, summarizing what they had read. The summaries were read and critiqued by two peers and then submitted to the teacher. Examples of two acceptable and two unacceptable summaries (written by the teacher) were prominently displayed on the bulletin board and the teacher discussed this in class at the beginning of the semester. Students with poor responses were asked to reexamine the examples on the bulletin board, comparing the acceptable responses to their own.

Modeling. Consistently display the behaviors others are expected to exhibit, both in words and actions.

Elementary example: The teacher explained to the targeted student that when he was feeling upset he was to come to her and say, "Ms. Greenwood, I need to talk with you; I am feeling upset (angry, frustrated, etc.)." He was to go on to say, "I really need to talk to you now." OR "I need to talk to you as soon as you can stop what you are doing." Ms. Greenwood demonstrated how to make this polite but urgent request by using the same technique with the student when she wanted to talk with him about either his negative or positive classroom behaviors. She was careful to vary instances of when she needed to talk to him immediately and when she could wait until it was a good time for him.

Secondary example: In a high school science class, the teacher referred to himself as Mr. Johnson and to the students by Miss or Mr. followed by their last name. He explained that this was a way of showing respect for one another and for respecting the learning environment. He explained to the students that they would be expected to address teachers, as well as one another, by title in this science class. No exceptions were made.

Structuring the situation. Arrange classroom conditions to produce desired behaviors.

Elementary example: Mrs. Cancionni, a fourth grade teacher, used cooperative learning groups for the reading of social studies lessons. Students took turns reading short passages to the groups and asking questions pertaining to the lesson. Andy was assigned to a group of two boys and one girl. All three were good students with acceptable classroom behaviors and leadership skills. The group gained points for lesson completion and acceptable group behavior. Andy also earned individual bonus points for the latter.

Secondary example: In Mr. Ruiz' American history class, students were expected to discuss readings and films in small discussion groups of four or five students. Reciprocal teaching (see Palincsar & Brown, 1984) was used where students took turns being the teacher and facilitating the discussion. Another student took turns taking notes on the major points of discussion, which were submitted to the teacher for group credit. All students took a turn as group facilitator and as group recorder. The groups were heterogeneously mixed by academic skill level.

Positive reinforcement.   Provide a stimulus that, when presented as a consequence of a response, results in an increase or maintenance of that response.

Elementary example: Justin was learning to take turns. It was very difficult for him to do and it was essential for being accepted in his kindergarten class. Every time he waited his turn, his teachers praised him for doing so.

Secondary example: Juliana was an eighth-grade student with reading and learning difficulties, reading three years below grade level. She had been taught to self-measure her oral and silent reading speeds (see Idol, 1997b). She recorded her speeds on a chart in her notebook. She took these measurements every day and set new benchmarks for gradually increasing her speed. She found the charting and responsibility to be rewarding and worked hard to read faster and faster.

Regulated permission.   Identify the likely impulse or motive behind a student's undesirable behavior and then find acceptable classroom alternatives for expression of this drive.

Elementary example: Danny was in the sixth grade and had been in a special education class for the previous 3 years. This was his first year in an inclusive classroom. After he had been in the class one week, his special education teacher visited the classroom to see how he was doing. When Danny saw her at the door he jumped out of his seat and walked across the tops of the desks in his row. The classroom teacher asked the special education teacher to leave and said she would handle Danny. At recess the special education teacher and Danny went for a walk. Danny revealed that he really missed his special education teacher and wanted to come back to the special education class. They talked about how difficult it is to make changes but that changes are required for growth and that Danny was growing in maturity and academically and how everyone wanted him to do well in his new class. The two teachers and Danny agreed he could come to the special education class over the lunch hour when the special education teacher was there just to talk, report his progress, and spend a little private time with his special education teacher. He remained successfully in this class.

Secondary example: Tina was insulting and rude to teachers. She acted like she did not care. When the teacher was talking, she rolled her eyes with disgust, fixed her makeup and hair, and mumbled surly remarks to other students. Tina and the teacher went to lunch at a nice, quiet restaurant where they could talk. In her own way, Tina revealed enough about her life that her teacher surmised that surliness and acting unconcerned was a way Tina had learned to survive and protect herself. Tina was given a credit hour for working with two girls in the program for students with severe disabilities, teaching them how to do their makeup and hair, and how to respond to their teacher with respect. Tina was encouraged for being a survivor and for teaching others to survive.

Contracting.   Establish a procedure for establishing a written and/or verbal agreement with one or more students to provide a particular service, reward, or outcome in return for a particular behavior or performance.

Elementary example: Amelia was a third-grade student who had difficulty getting along with other students. She fought with other girls, speaking quite meanly and harshly to them. Amelia and her teacher agreed that for every day she did not fight, and played or studied agreeably with at least one different person each week, she could help with copying papers in the staff office. She had asked previously if she could do this work, so it was motivating for her. The contract was a verbal one between Amelia, her classroom teacher, the principal, and the principal's assistant.

Secondary example: Andy was a 10th-grade student who expressed interest in doing extra reading at home and suggested that his mother could be his tutor. At the time, he was enrolled in a reading support course in his high school, where all students were required to take a basic reading course. Students were required to repeat this course until they demonstrated mastery. Credit was received each term. The program was offered by the resource/consulting teacher, Mr. Davis. He telephoned Andy's mother and set up a short meeting with her and Andy. In the meeting, they developed a contract that all three signed stating the conditions of the home study program, with Andy assuming managerial responsibilities. His mother wanted a stipulation in the contract that (a) Andy would take responsibility for arranging the tutoring sessions and (b) if Andy's mother had to assume managerial responsibilities (i.e., nagging Andy to do his reading or gathering the materials), then the home tutoring project would be terminated. Andy made 2.85 months gain per month of instruction for the two months he and his mother worked together (see Idol, 1993, pp. 262–265).

Token system.   Use tangible objects or symbols that can be exchanged for a privilege, activity, or reward.

Elementary example: David was old enough to be in fourth grade, had severe learning disabilities and related behavior problems, and had been in self-contained special education classes since he was 7 years old. He worked hard in the special education program to learn his multiplication tables and to perform basic calculations in addition, subtraction, multiplication, and division. The school principal made the decision to include David in a third-grade math class for his first general classroom experience since the first grade. His third-grade teacher used candy reinforcers for all students in the class. The candy was in a large jar on her desk and students received candy for numbers of math problems completed correctly with appropriate accompanying social behavior. David found this highly motivating, demanding to know why candy was not given in the special education class! No candy was ever given in the special education class as the teachers wanted David to want to be in general education. Over the next 2 years, his experiences in general education were gradually increased so that by the time he was in fifth grade, he was fully included.

Secondary example: Earning points is an example of the use of symbolic tokens, if the points are traded in for specific rewards. In Michael's sixth-grade math class at a middle school, students earned points for completion of different types of math assignments. Unlike most students, Michael also earned points for appropriate classroom behavior—he could earn opportunities to go with a group of students to Mr. Gatti's Pizzeria (a school adopter) for lunch.

Reducing Undesirable Behaviors

Planned ignoring. Ignore or tolerate undesirable behavior so that it will drop out or be extinguished.

Elementary example: Eduardo was a fourth-grade student who suffered from paranoia and other emotional problems. He did not like to go anywhere because he thought people were staring at him. This fear extended to his not wanting to go outside of his classroom, to the playground, down the hall, or to the cafeteria. He did not have friends and had been in a self-contained special education program since the beginning of second grade. He was very bright and had taught himself to read prior to entering the first grade. He was enrolled in a resource transition program intended to support Eduardo in eventually returning to a general classroom.

The resource room teacher, Ms. Fleming, decided that ignoring Eduardo would be a good way to help him gradually become more comfortable with groups of people and in various settings. Thus, when Eduardo entered the classroom or moved about in the classroom or walked with other resource students to various places in the school, Ms. Fleming was careful not to look at him. She always waited for Eduardo to initiate contact with her prior to looking at him. When Eduardo asked, she would reply, "Oh, I wasn't looking at you, Eduardo." This ignoring strategy worked well, with Eduardo initiating more contact with his teacher and beginning to accept invitations from other students to venture outside of the resource room. Two years later, Eduardo was included fully in a fifth-grade classroom. Inclusion of Eduardo was a gradual, challenging, and carefully planned process. Ignoring worked well in dealing with his paranoia, but it was only one of many different techniques that were used with this student.

Secondary example: Philip, an eighth-grade student, was the master of surliness. His usual stance and demeanor suggested this message: "I am a tough guy, so you'd better watch out!" He maintained this stance with adults and peers. Many teachers engaged in confrontation with Philip because they reacted to this stance and demanded a change in his behavior.

Then Philip met Miss Hurley, his third-period science teacher. Miss Hurley talked to Philip, gave him classroom instruction, asked him questions, made the usual teacher demands of him. She treated him like any other student she liked and simply ignored his surly behavior. For a while, his demeanor would appear even more fierce, but Miss Hurley was undaunted. She continued to ignore his "tough guy" act and to expect the best from Philip. Philip began to soften. He began to make an exception for Miss Hurley. When questioned by other students about his shift in response to Miss Hurley, he said, "She's different. Miss Hurley, she cares. She's not like them others."

Stating expectations. Clearly establish individual classroom behavior expectations, preferably arrived at with student input and agreement.

Elementary example: When Eduardo (described in the above example) was included in a fifth-grade classroom, his teacher, Mr. Love, was very clear in his expectations for Eduardo. Mr. Love told Eduardo that he expected him to be like all the other boys in the class. He expected Eduardo to walk up to his desk if he needed help, complete assignments during the class time, and to answer when asked questions.

These are usual and simple classroom expectations, but for Eduardo the first two of these behaviors were difficult to execute. In the resource room he didn't always ask for help when needed, and usually did not complete assignments on time because he worked too slowly and was too perfectionistic. He had learned to respond appropriately to teacher questions. Mr. Love asked Eduardo if he was capable of making these responses. To the special education teacher's surprise, Eduardo's response was affirmative. Then Mr. Love made it very clear that if Eduardo chose not to respond in these three appropriate ways, he could not be in his class. By this time, Eduardo really wanted to be in a fifth-grade class and be just like all the other students. So, Eduardo agreed to try to meet Mr. Love's expectations, and most of the time he did.

Secondary example: Mr. Castle decided to use cooperative learning groups in his American history class. Each group would be responsible for taking a time span in history and creating a multimedia project to be used to teach the rest of the class. The students and Mr. Castle brainstormed a list of behavior expectations for the cooperative learning group and for individuals within each group. The expectations were for social behavior as well as for learning behavior and academic performance. Then, the entire group went back over the list, discussing the pros and cons for each possible expectation. Eventually, the group reached consensus on those expectations that everyone, Mr. Castle and each of the students, could accept.

Signaling.   Use nonverbal signals to curb negative behaviors.

Elementary example: In Mrs. Carter's class, the Assertive Discipline Program was used (Canter & Canter, 1982) with all students. A student's name was written on the board the first time a student violated a classroom rule. A check mark was placed by the student's name each of the next three times the rule was violated in the same day. If the rule was violated again, it was understood by all that the student would be removed from the classroom. For each of these violations, Mrs. Carter said nothing. She simply wrote the names, made the check marks, and then called the assistant principal for immediate student removal for the fifth violation.

Secondary example: In biology class Mr. Furtado found that using nonverbal signaling was a powerful way to prompt and correct students' misbehaviors without embarrassing them or drawing undue attention to them. Mr. Furtado realized that adolescents are particularly vulnerable to public embarrassment and eager to maintain a sense of "coolness" in the presence of their peers. Mr. Furtado and Raul developed a nonverbal communication system that was private to the two of them. The signals consisted of Mr. Furtado pulling his right ear to indicate that Raul was not listening to teacher directions, extending his thumb from his fist in an upward direction to indicate that Raul was behaving or working well, and placing his index and middle fingers in a V-shape and touching the middle finger to the outside corner of his eye to indicate that Raul needed to "watch out" (meaning that he was very close to being in trouble with Mr. Furtado). Mr. Furtado was careful to send these signals when other students were not looking.

Restructuring. Regulate the level of classroom disruption by restructuring or modifying the situation to bolster behavior control and attenuate stress.

Elementary example: In Ms. Anders's third-grade class, a classroom system was developed for when the students became disruptive or the noise level got too high. Ms. Anders would turn the classroom lights off. This was a signal for everyone to stop what they were doing, stand up where they were, turn their faces toward the classroom clock, and watch the second hand make a 1-minute revolution of the clock. The class called it "Stopping Time."

Secondary example: In Mr. Henson's eighth-grade class, it became increasingly apparent that many students had difficulty staying on task with the language arts lesson for the entire 90 minutes that were allotted. This was especially true for five very active boys. Mr. Henson broke the class into five small groups and distributed the active boys across the groups. The language arts lesson was divided into four segments: read independently, read with the small group, write a summary with an assigned partner of what was read, and take a structured, free time break if all three tasks were completed.

Conferencing. Arrange a private conference with a problem student to exchange views in a confidential manner and to help the student see your concerns.

Elementary example: Ginny was in first grade and had difficulty with wetting her pants at school. Her teacher, Mrs. Wilson, and Ginny spent a recess together, sitting under a pecan tree and having a little snack. They talked about what to do about this problem. They decided to have an extra set of panties and shorts in the teacher's desk for emergencies. They also decided that they would set a small timer on Mrs. Wilson's desk. When it went off, Mrs. Wilson would turn it off and say nothing. If other students asked, she would say it was to help remind her of something. When the timer went off, Ginny would stop what she was doing and leave quietly to go to the bathroom. If other students questioned Ginny's leaving, they would be told quietly that Ginny had permission to leave.

Secondary example: Charles and his basketball coach met alone after practice without the knowledge of the other players. They discussed how Charles lost his temper so easily on the court. They talked about how the team needed Charles as the strong and consistent player he was; not as being constantly "fouled out" for his temper outbursts. The coach told Charles that the ball was literally in his court. The coach emphasized how temper and anger can interfere with one's life, both personally and professionally. He said the team needed Charles and that Charles needed to decide if he was going to control this temper monster or let it interfere with his life now and probably in the future as well.

Warning. Establish consequences for undesirable behavior in advance of enforcement.

Elementary example: Kirsten was in third grade. She whined, which caused students to shun her and which irritated her teacher, Mr. Bradley. Mr. Bradley agreed to let Kirsten help straighten the classroom if she did not whine in class. Kirsten wanted to help after school for about 10 minutes while waiting for her mother. Her mother was single and Kirsten seemed to need some adult male attention.

If Kirsten started to whine, Mr. Bradley said, "Are we going to keep our agreement?" This was his way of warning Kirsten that the whining must stop, or the agreement for the 10-minute work period would be canceled.

Secondary example: Ms. Woodley taught 11th-grade English literature and was often frustrated with Kevin because he was smart, read well, wrote acceptably, and had potential for succeeding in English literature. However, Kevin was a procrastinator. He visited with other students, daydreamed, read other materials, and fiddled around after classroom assignments were given. Ms. Woodley, concerned that Kevin would not be able to go to college if he kept up his procrastinating, spoke with him, and Kevin said that he did want to go to college. Together, they obtained a scholarship commitment from a local church for Kevin to attend community college upon graduation. Kevin wanted to succeed; he just couldn't seem to get started on the tasks to be done.

Ms. Woodley agreed to write Kevin a small note and slip it to him when he was procrastinating. The notes said such things as "College?" "Does the smart man go on?" "Do obstacles obstruct the man with a purpose?" and "????". The notes varied, were thoughtful and probing, and sometimes funny. The notes were the warnings that connected Kevin to a much bigger outcome—one in which Kevin had a vested interest.

Enforcement of consequences. Follow through on announced consequences for unacceptable behavior. The consequences should be immediate, nonpunitive, and consistent.

Elementary example: Ryan had difficulty playing with others in his kindergarten class. He wanted to interact with other students and be a part of small groups, but he hit other children, grabbed toys out of their hands, and called other children rude names. The class was organized so that children rotated in small groups through various learning and activity centers.

Ryan's teacher, Mrs. Bentley, explained to Ryan that he could rotate with various groups and interact in the activities as long as he shared and behaved nicely with others. If he did not behave appropriately, Mrs. Bentley took him to a small rug on the floor, near her, where he had to sit alone for a few minutes. He was then allowed to rejoin the group. Mrs. Bentley made no exceptions to this intervention. If Ryan hit, grabbed toys, or called names, he was immediately guided to the rug.

Secondary example: At one high school, there were problems with gangs, with some gang members bringing weapons to school. The district implemented a policy that any student bringing weapons to school would be immediately expelled from school. Reentry in an alternative school program required the student to attend at least 10 supportive counseling sessions. Reentry in the local high school was only possible after completion of counseling, completion of required coursework at the alternative high school, and development and implementation of a transition plan by a team of educators, parents, and the student. No exceptions were made. Weapons at school resulted in immediate expulsion.

Crisis intervention. Engage in immediate intervention when a student is a threat to self or others.

Elementary example: Robert and Jason were both in fifth grade (assigned to two different classes) and attended the elementary school described earlier in this chapter. Both of these boys were extremely difficult to manage in classrooms. When crisis intervention was made possible for these two boys, the entire faculty became much more willing to include other students with learning and/or milder behavior problems.

All teachers knew Robert and Jason and had encountered their problems at various levels and places within the building.

A crisis intervention program was implemented in each of their classes. Assertive discipline was used, as described earlier. The boys, as well as any student in the class, received four nonverbal warnings prior to removal from the classroom. Removal from the classroom occurred under either of two conditions: (a) if the student had received four warnings or (b) if the student attempted bodily harm or assault to any other person in the classroom. If either of these occurred, the teacher signaled the teacher next door to watch over the class and took the student directly to the assistant principal's office. If the student refused to go, the teacher telephoned the vice principal, who came to get the student.

In this school, because disruptive behavior was relatively common, the primary responsibility of the assistant principal was to support teachers when behavior problems occurred. There was a school policy that either the vice principal or the counselor would be present in the building at all times. The counselor served as a backup for the vice principal.

Secondary example: At a middle school, the counselors were responsible for crisis intervention. The principal served as support on an as-needed basis by her choice. There were three counselors, one for each of the three grade levels: sixth, seventh, and eighth grades. After three warnings, the first level of intervention was for the student to meet with the parents and teachers and discuss the classroom behavior problems.

The student was removed from the classroom if disruptions continued after this point, or if the student was dangerous to self or others. Either could result in removal from the classroom. The teacher telephoned the counseling office via the school intercom system, and any one of the three counselors came directly to the classroom, taking the student to the counseling office to discuss what had occurred. This was followed up with a meeting with the counselor, the counselor assigned to the student's grade level if a different counselor had to intervene, the student, the teacher, and the parents.

Summary

In this chapter emphasis was placed on creating equality in the classroom, respecting the rights of everyone, creating learning environments that are safe, and teachers supporting rather than punishing students, helping other staff members, and involving parents and guardians in intervention plans for students. Collaborators are encouraged to use a decision-making framework, Levels of Intensity of Intervention for Effective Student Management, to aid them in selecting appropriate interventions for students who are troubled or troubling. The various types of interventions that are described within the framework are then defined, with examples provided for application in both elementary and secondary schools.

CHAPTER SEVEN

◆ ◆ ◆ ◆ ◆ ◆ ◆ ◆ ◆ ◆ ◆ ◆ ◆ ◆ ◆ ◆ ◆

Do Teachers Need To Change How They Teach in Inclusive Classrooms?

◆ There seem to be two major, looming fears classroom teachers have about inclusion. One is that they would have to change completely how they teach. The second is that the student with challenging needs would take up an inordinate amount of the classroom teacher's time. The feared result would be that the other students in the class would be deprived of rightful teacher attention.

One of the significant keys to successful inclusion is to design and implement instructional adaptations that allow students with special challenges to be taught, as much as possible, with a larger group of students. In some instances, teachers may actually find themselves changing from how they have taught in the past. But in many more instances, teachers realize that they have already made a lot of instructional adaptations for certain students and that many of these same adaptations would be appropriate for the student with challenging needs. In this realization, they begin to overcome their fears that any student with a special education label is very difficult to teach and requires a very specialized teaching methodology in order to learn. This is a very commonly held myth by classroom teachers, especially by those opposed to inclusion.

Types of Instructional Adaptations

In this chapter we will explore a variety of instructional adaptations that have been used successfully by many teachers in inclusive classrooms. These teachers have been a part of teacher education staff development programs where they worked in collaborative teams (comprised of both classroom and special education teachers) to generate a list of various types of instructional adaptations they have used successfully. I provided them with a framework for organizing the various adaptations (see Figure 7.1), which was used for listing the various adaptations by type.

The framework is organized into five categories, as described by Lewis and Doorlag (1991) and Idol and West (1993). The five categories are described as follows. For each there is a corresponding appendix that provides a list of various examples of that particular type of adaptation.

Instructional Activities and Materials	Teaching Procedures	Task Requirements (Same Task)	Alternative Task Selection (Same Curriculum)	Alternative Task Selection (Different Curriculum)

Figure 7.1. Instructional adaptations matrix.

Instructional Activities and Materials: An adaptation in any tasks and/or using any type of media or tools for learning (see Appendix 7.A).

Teaching Procedures: An adaptation in any way that actual teaching takes place in the classroom. This could be instruction led by teachers, assistants, students, parents, or computers (see Appendix 7.B).

Task Requirements (Same Task): An adaptation in the requirements for the student with challenges, even though the task itself is the same as that assigned to other students (see Appendix 7.C).

Alternative Task Selection (Same Curriculum): An adaptation in the actual task the student with challenges is doing. The other students in the class are engaged in a different task, but all students are working within the same curriculum (see Appendix 7.D).

Alternative Task Selection (Different Curriculum): An adaptation in both the task the student with challenges is doing, as well as offering the student a different curriculum than the one used with the other students in the class (see Appendix 7.E).

Adaptations or changes can be made in any aspect of the teaching and learning process as reflected by these five categories. As seen in Figure 7.1, the categories are listed from the easiest to implement (instructional activities and materials) to the most difficult to implement (alternative task selection—different curriculum).

It is important to appreciate the distinctions among the five columns. Sometimes when teachers are resistive to making adaptations, they believe any adaptation is very difficult, requires extra adults to implement, and necessitates offering more than one curriculum simultaneously. Clarity on the distinctions among the columns helps us to realize that many of the adaptations in the first three columns are relatively easy to implement and can be done by a single teacher. The column distinctions can also help us be more selective in the adaptations we choose so that we truly do select those that are relatively easy to implement while still ensuring student success.

When teachers are asked to use these five columns for categorizing the various types of adaptations they have used, four important concepts are conveyed:

1. Teachers realize they already know of and are using many adaptations.

2. Teachers often realize they do not need a special course or special education certification to make adaptations.

3. Teachers realize they do not need a significant amount of special education support to implement adaptations in the classroom.

4. Teachers learn from each other several adaptations that others have been using but that are new to them.

What Do You Already Know About Making Adaptations?

Like the teachers described above, it is important for you to realize how much you, too, already know about making adaptations in the classroom for students with special challenges. Before reading any further, please stop and reflect on what you already know. Use Figure 7.1 to make your notations. Use a brainstorming process and simply list the various adaptations you have already used in your own teaching. List the ideas as they come to you, writing them down in the column you believe most accurately describes the adaptation.

You could also do this activity with a colleague or with your collaborative team. Of course, completing the activity with others will result in a longer and richer list, and you will have already engaged in a mutual teaching and learning process. Once again, you will appreciate the greater capacity for both quality and quantity of production when a team comes together to work.

When you have finished with the brainstorming, look over the completed form. Which are the columns that are easiest for you to implement in your classroom? Or, which columns are best to use with a particular classroom teacher with whom you are working? Do you have more ideas listed in the first three columns than in the last two columns? This is likely the case. And this is important to realize as well: Many of the adaptations we make in classrooms have to do with the activities and materials we use, the ways we teach, or the tasks we require of our students.

Yet, for many of us, when we think about making adaptations for a student with special challenges, we automatically conclude that the adaptations would require making significant changes—such as changes in the tasks within a curriculum; working at a lower level in the curriculum; or having to offer a separate curriculum to the special student. This is not always the case; rather, it is much more likely that the lesser types of adaptations will be sufficient for many students with learning challenges.

Outside Influences on Making Adaptations

First, you should examine Appendixes 7.A through 7.E and generate your own list of classroom adaptations. Consider also that several outside influences will impact how extensive the adaptations will be in a successful, inclusive classroom.

Following is a discussion of nine such influences that I have found to affect the amount of adaptation that actually occurs in the inclusive classroom.

Student performance level versus the classroom instructional standard. Some teachers set a single, high standard for all students regardless of whether all students can reach the standard. Some teachers set a medium-level standard, expecting that some students will meet the standard, some will surpass it, and some will never achieve it. In inclusive classrooms, teachers work in teams to set multiple standards for different levels of students: those who consistently surpass teacher expectation, those who are (with proper support) capable of mastering grade-level standards, those who will master a core set of basic skills, and those who will be working on a social skill development or supportive lifestyle curriculum.

Teachers' skills in adapting both curriculum and instruction. Of course, the degree of skills possessed by the classroom teacher and the collaborating team impact greatly on the amount and quality of adaptations made in the inclusive classroom. As emphasized earlier in this chapter, classroom teachers often think they know less about making classroom adaptations than they actually do. Special education teachers often fear that they don't know enough about the general education curriculum to make adaptations. When special and general educators work together in teams—thus benefiting from one another's knowledge—they are able to implement much more successful adaptations.

Number of students with learning and/or behavior problems in the classroom. This is an important issue to consider when including students with special education problems who require adaptations in curriculum and instruction. First, if the classroom teacher can use the same adaptations with other students with learning and/or behavior problems in the classroom, he or she is usually more likely to implement the adaptations.

However, if the proportion of students with learning and/or behavior problems is very high, the classroom teacher may feel too overwhelmed to consider any adaptations. The teacher in this situation generally feels that it takes all available energy to "simply make it through the day." It is this classroom condition, though, that is actually the most ripe for developing adaptations in curriculum and instruction because relief is needed so badly in the classroom.

Finally, if the proportions of students with learning and behavior problems vary greatly from class to class, then it is very likely necessary to create more equitable balances in these proportions across the classes. Inequitable proportions lend themselves to strife and discontent among the faculty. Righting the proportions contributes to developing a sense that the entire faculty is working together to build a collaborative and inclusive school. The reader is reminded of the intermediate school faculty described in Chapter 1 who agreed to balance inequitable proportions as their first step toward inclusion.

Type and scope of school support services available. The more supported the classroom teacher, the more likely it is that curricular and instructional adaptations will be implemented. (See Chapter 4 for a description of providing support services to classroom teachers.)

Existence of a quality, collaborative planning and problem-solving process. Teams of people working together collaboratively create classroom adaptations that simply do not occur when people are working in isolation. Two heads are truly better than one. (See Chapter 5 for an explanation of what a quality-based planning and problem-solving process should look like.)

Legitimate time to consult.   Regardless of the type of support provided to the classroom teacher, time to consult is essential in the development of quality adaptations that are appropriate and well conceptualized. As classroom teachers become more confident in implementing adaptations, the time needed may decrease. In the beginning, however, sufficient time is essential to program development. (See Chapter 3 for a list of various ways that faculty in collaborative and inclusive schools have found more time for consulting with one another.)

Availability of adapted instructional materials.   As teachers and assistants work more and more together, they develop larger and larger repertoires of adaptations. They also become more skilled in knowing how intensive, time consuming, and practical the various adaptations are. They create certain types of adaptations that are in physical form, such as tape-recorded texts, tests, materials, and instructions; highlighted textbooks and materials; adapted tests; multimedia approaches to instruction; learning centers; written guidelines for peer buddy and tutoring systems; and a variety of other adaptations of a more permanent nature. As this pool of resources enlarges, so does the receptivity of classroom teachers to the idea of implementing adaptations in their classrooms.

School staff support for education in the most enabling and productive instructional environment.   Teachers in buildings where the administrators have taken a positive stance on inclusion and collaboration are more likely to make adaptations. This is particularly true if it really is a collaborative school where all have been involved in the decision-making process that led to creating a school-wide vision focusing on all children learning and all children being enabled to be as productive and achieving as possible.

Idol's Nine Simple Rules for Making Adaptations

Finally, in my years of working with collaborative teams, nine simple rules for making adaptations have surfaced:

1. Keep it simple. Complicated adaptations rarely stay in place over time.

2. Use the classroom curriculum whenever possible. It is a grave disservice to students to prevent them from learning in the classroom curriculum unless absolutely unavoidable. Also, classroom teachers are much less likely to change or adapt the curriculum than they are to adapt activities, materials, teaching procedures, and student performance standards.

3. Select adaptations that are useful with several other students in the classroom. An adaptation that can be used with several other students is more effective and practical for teaching large groups of students.

4. Select adaptations that promote student independence and responsibility for learning. When students learn to take responsibility for their own learning, much less demand is placed on the classroom teacher. Perhaps more importantly, the student has been given a gift for life.

5. Select adaptations that encourage generalization in learning. Often, students with more moderate learning problems need direct teaching in the generalization of learned concepts to different situations and settings. It is when students can generalize what they

have learned that they have truly learned, as opposed to learning by rote for immediate and short-term performance.

6. Consider the necessary labor effort. Highly labor-intensive adaptations are usually not actually implemented (or if implemented, last only for a short time). This is because the demands on the classroom teacher are heavy and multi-faceted.

7. Consider how time consuming the adaptation is to implement. An adaptation that takes an inordinate amount of classroom time and supports only a small portion of what is needed for the student to succeed is not likely to be effective. A balance should be kept between the class time needed for the adaptation and the payoff for using the adaptation.

8. Start with the least intensive adaptations. If an adaptation in instructional activities and materials—the least intensive type of adaptation—will solve the problem, there is no need to go further.

9. Select adaptations that are culturally relevant. It is important for students to understand why they are learning the material. When they do not, they often describe the learning as "boring." When the learning environment and related student activities are supportive of the surrounding culture, it is often easier for students to see the relevance of their learning.

Summary

In answer to the question posed as the title for this chapter, teachers really do not need to change as much as they sometimes think they do. They know a great deal about how to create adapted learning environments. When they work in collaborative teams, they teach one another even more about what they know. Making informed and intelligent choices in selecting appropriate adaptations is an essential part of the collaborative team process. Making distinctions among levels of intensity of adaptations, considering the impact of outside influences, and following successful and simple rules for using adaptations can increase the likelihood of creating inclusive classrooms where all students are learning at a maximal level.

APPENDIX 7.A
Examples of Adaptations in Instructional Activities and Materials

_____ 1. Provide student with a copy of class notes

_____ 2. Provide NCR paper

_____ 3. Conduct oral testing

_____ 4. Let student take tape-recorded class notes

_____ 5. Use lower-level textbooks for certain students

_____ 6. Use a variety of difficulty levels of reading materials

_____ 7. Underline the verbs in written directions

_____ 8. Let student use a calculator to complete the task requirements

_____ 9. Brainstorm in discussion before writing an essay

_____ 10. Set up preferential seating

_____ 11. Provide instructional games and puzzles

_____ 12. Tape-record a book chapter

_____ 13. Give instructor lecture notes to a student

_____ 14. Give a student study guides and reference sheets

_____ 15. Let student do a computerized drill, practice, and review

_____ 16. Allow a peer to take notes for a student

_____ 17. Provide different activities organized by various learning styles of students

_____ 18. Videotape instruction (for independent student review)

_____ 19. Use concrete manipulatives

_____ 20. Highlight important parts of text

_____ 21. Let student use spell check on the computer for essays

_____ 22. Fold a paper in half to shorten an assignment

_____ 23. Let student make charts to demonstrate understanding

_____ 24. Encourage use of rulers and tape measures as a number line

_____ 25. Provide a guide for reading materials

_____ 26. Select some materials for enlarging the print

_____ 27. Establish learning centers

_____ 28. Expand academic assignments to include artwork

_____ 29. Let student use headphones

_____ 30. Create concrete, whole-body activities

© 2002 by PRO-ED, Inc.

———— 31. Requisition special equipment (adaptive devices)

———— 32. Let student use calculators

———— 33. Requisition science learning kits with a hands-on approach

———— 34. Teach students to use a word processor

———— 35. Require student to establish word banks

———— 36. Use cooperative learning groups

———— 37. Provide alternative materials—lined paper, graph paper, etc.

———— 38. Use flash cards

———— 39. Provide decks of cards for counting, sorting, and categorizing

———— 40. Display posters for concepts, procedures, etc.

———— 41. Offer word-search activities

———— 42. Require journal writing

———— 43. Offer multiple-choice testing

———— 44. Let student demonstrate learning by oral reports to a peer buddy

———— 45. Encourage small group discussions

———— 46. Utilize small, flexible groups for skill drills

———— 47. Request kinesthetic materials

———— 48. Clarify or shorten written directions in materials

———— 49. Add prompts or cues to the learner task

———— 50. Use a variety of learning activities (e.g., expository, inquiry, demonstrations)

———— 51. Use peer assistants

———— 52. Encourage a student with limited physical ability to hold instruments or tools in mouth

———— 53. Provide guide ropes for students with visual impairments to follow

———— 54. Use a variety of types of rhythm instruments that all children can manipulate

———— 55. Use a slant table or clipboards

———— 56. Provide crossword puzzles with and without word lists

———— 57. Utilize laminated materials

———— 58. Use controlled, environmental sounds to guide student movement from activity to activity

———— 59. _____

———— 60. _____

———— 61. _____

———— 62. _____

———— 63. _____

© 2002 by PRO-ED, Inc.

APPENDIX 7.B
Examples of Adaptations in Teaching Procedures

_____ 1. Give additional presentation of skills and concept information

_____ 2. Provide additional guided practice

_____ 3. Make rewards for successful performance more attractive

_____ 4. Change the pace of instruction

_____ 5. Reduce the quantity of information presented in a given instructional lesson

_____ 6. Use cooperative teaching

_____ 7. Give the directions in a student's native language

_____ 8. Provide visual cues

_____ 9. Enhance lectures with visual presentations

_____ 10. Use peer tutoring

_____ 11. Practice flexible ability grouping of students

_____ 12. Implement cooperative learning groups

_____ 13. Provide individualized instruction

_____ 14. Include prereading activities

_____ 15. Use sign language

_____ 16. Provide discovery learning opportunities

_____ 17. Provide compare-contrast learning opportunities

_____ 18. Teach using both examples and nonexamples of concept to be taught

_____ 19. Offer students opportunities to interpret and evaluate what they have learned

_____ 20. Teach critical-thinking skills

_____ 21. Teach students to outline when reading and listening

_____ 22. Use panel groups for instruction

_____ 23. Modify and expand oral directions

_____ 24. Use rephrasing and paraphrasing

_____ 25. Provide oral prompts

_____ 26. Illustrate sequential steps

_____ 27. Use the overhead projector

_____ 28. Use the chalkboard

_____ 29. Provide learning bulletin boards

_____ 30. Display numerals and timelines

© 2002 by PRO-ED, Inc.

_____ 31. Utilize small group instruction

_____ 32. Use flexible, skill drill groups

_____ 33. Incorporate art, music, and physical activity with academic instruction

_____ 34. Provide students with vocabulary words to store in word banks

_____ 35. Use a variety of visual and auditory presentations

_____ 36. Conduct individualized student progress assessments

_____ 37. Facilitate student learning

_____ 38. State the learning objectives

_____ 39. Model the skills and behaviors you want the students to use

_____ 40. Monitor student learning

_____ 41. Give dictation as a means of teaching students to follow directions

_____ 42. Combine both verbal and written instructions

_____ 43. Give both oral and written tests

_____ 44. Let students translate for other students

_____ 45. Utilize an interpreter for students with hearing impairments

_____ 46. Provide re-teaching and review opportunities for small, flexible groups

_____ 47. Assign peer buddies

_____ 48. Provide frequent feedback on student performance

_____ 49. Provide role-playing opportunities

_____ 50. Let students teach each other and the class

_____ 51. Teach one objective at a time

_____ 52. Use a multi-sensory approach to teaching

_____ 53. Monitor student progress during practice sessions

_____ 54. Provide direct, individualized teaching when errors are made

_____ 55. Use instructional assistants

_____ 56. Have students read with a partner

_____ 57. Utilize peer tutoring

_____ 58. Enlarge visual aids

_____ 59. Provide students with a list of questions so they will be prepared to listen to lectures

_____ 60. Use nonverbal cues to alert or guide certain students

_____ 61. Lower the readability level of the major textbook used

_____ 62. Use parent and community volunteers

_____ 63. Define limits of behavior

© 2002 by PRO-ED, Inc.

_____ 64. Give routine breaks/rests

_____ 65. Use reinforcers and rewards consistently

_____ 66. Use checklists to monitor behavior

_____ 67. Use a behavior management plan

_____ 68. Use multi-colored pens and chalk

_____ 69. Use prerecorded stories and headphones

_____ 70. Use computerized instruction for initial instruction or presenting new information

_____ 71. Use money to aid in teaching counting, sorting, and counting in base 5 and 10 systems

_____ 72. Use an abacus to teach place value and basic math functions

_____ 73. _____

_____ 74. _____

_____ 75. _____

_____ 76. _____

_____ 77. _____

© 2002 by PRO-ED, Inc.

APPENDIX 7.C
Examples of Adaptations in Task Requirements
(Same Task)

_____ 1. Increase the amount of time for work completion for some students

_____ 2. Increase the amount of response time for some students

_____ 3. Shorten or reduce assignments

_____ 4. Change the performance criteria

_____ 5. Change the characteristics of the task (e.g., nature of task conditions or response mode)

_____ 6. Break each task into smaller subtasks

_____ 7. Use differential grading

_____ 8. Provide oral testing

_____ 9. Show students where to find the answer

_____ 10. Let students answer on a recording machine rather than in writing

_____ 11. Let a peer record answers

_____ 12. Increase gradually task requirements

_____ 13. Provide testing with no time limit

_____ 14. Give partial credit

_____ 15. Use individualized performance criteria

_____ 16. Read shorter selections

_____ 17. Assign only the even-numbered math problems

_____ 18. Delete the more challenging cognitive questions for slower students

_____ 19. Let a student just learning to spell write only the beginning sounds/letters

_____ 20. Let a student take oral spelling tests

_____ 21. Use a calculator for math problems

_____ 22. Shorten spelling word lists

_____ 23. Shorten reading assignments

_____ 24. Write a smaller number of paragraphs

_____ 25. Write the assignment on the computer instead of by hand

_____ 26. Let some students learn the basic steps of the Texas two-step while others learn to combine steps with twirls, swings, and passes

_____ 27. _____

_____ 28. _____

_____ 29. _____

_____ 30. _____

_____ 31. _____

© 2002 by PRO-ED, Inc.

APPENDIX 7.D
Examples of Adaptations by Alternative Task Selection (Same Curriculum)

———— 1. Select a similar, but easier, task

———— 2. Select a prerequisite task for the same curriculum

———— 3. Draw pictures, charts, and illustrations instead of writing

———— 4. Use audio materials of the same curriculum

———— 5. Use alternative tests

———— 6. Select a core and basic curriculum within the entire curriculum

———— 7. Use artwork and physical demonstrations to illustrate understanding

———— 8. Let a student dictate answers to the teacher or a peer

———— 9. Give a different test with fewer details

———— 10. Simplify the task

———— 11. Have students do a "hands-on" project

———— 12. Allow a student to fill in an outline/advanced organizer

———— 13. Provide a list of possible answers

———— 14. Use cloze procedure to check for understanding

———— 15. Establish learning labs

———— 16. Simplify math problems

———— 17. Provide an easier level of the same worksheet

———— 18. Provide highlighted text

———— 19. Modify a form for lab write-ups

———— 20. Place a student in a lower-level book in the same curriculum

———— 21. Make audio or electronic books available instead of literature books of the same story

———— 22. Let students work at different levels of difficulty within the same subject

———— 23. Let a student locate states and capitals on a map, rather than memorizing them

———— 24. Let a student throw a ball against the wall instead of making baskets

———— 25. Let a student record an oral story while other students are writing stories

———— 26. Provide adapted textbooks

———— 27. _____

———— 28. _____

———— 29. _____

———— 30. _____

© 2002 by PRO-ED, Inc.

APPENDIX 7.E
Examples of Adaptations by Alternative Task Selection (Different Curriculum)

_____ 1. Select an appropriate task from an alternative curriculum or program

_____ 2. Offer a social skills program to a lower-functioning student while other students are simultaneously engaged in an academic program

_____ 3. Let a student work on sorting and categorizing while other students solve math problems

_____ 4. Let a student work on a computer program that is unrelated to what other students are studying

_____ 5. Provide high-interest, low-level reading materials

_____ 6. Provide textbooks on the subject but at different grade levels

_____ 7. Let a student work on shape discrimination while other students are counting money

_____ 8. Let a student sort pictures to classify animals while other students are studying the food chain

_____ 9. Let some students work on counting while other students are working long division problems

_____ 10. Allow some students to be responsible for ensuring lab safety rules are followed while others read the content of the science lab manual

_____ 11. Let some students design the physical organization of a legislative session while others prepare a piece of proposed legislation

_____ 12. Let a student count jumps while other students are jumping rope

_____ 13. Modify the activity and content due to religious differences

_____ 14. _____

_____ 15. _____

_____ 16. _____

_____ 17. _____

_____ 18. _____

© 2002 by PRO-ED, Inc.

CHAPTER EIGHT

Is It Possible for Students To Learn at Different Levels and Rates in Inclusive Classrooms?

◆ Most educators and parents are concerned that inclusion of a student with special needs will impede the learning of the other students in the classroom. The primary reason for a collaborative school to offer a variety of ways of supporting classroom teachers is to ensure that this does not happen and that all students have an opportunity to learn. This chapter features use of cooperative learning groups and multi-layered lessons. Both are demonstrations of how various students in a heterogeneous class can be learning at different levels and rates.

Use of cooperative learning groups forms the basic structure for designing multi-layered lessons. The purpose of multi-layered lessons is to accommodate students of varying skill levels. The purposes for use of cooperative learning groups are as follows:

- to build a heterogenous learning structure that enables students to learn from each other;
- to learn cooperatively rather than competitively; and
- to accommodate students with special learning and behavior challenges within the group structure.

Cooperative Learning Groups

The effects of cooperative learning as an instructional methodology have been well researched and documented. The interested reader may want to refer to several comprehensive and detailed reviews of literature (Johnson & Johnson, 1987; Johnson, Maruyama, Johnson, Nelson, & Skon, 1981; Sharan, 1980; Slavin, 1984). The research findings support the use of cooperative learning in the following areas of cognition:

- increased academic achievement;
- higher retention;
- higher levels of thinking (e.g., analytic reasoning);
- more varied strategies to solve problems;
- increased use of metacognitive strategies; and
- increased frequency of new ideas.

TABLE 8.1
Cooperative Learning in the Classroom: Implementation Procedure

Step 1: Determine the objective(s).

Step 2: Specify the group sizes and assign students to the groups.

Step 3: Arrange the classroom.

Step 4: Provide the appropriate materials.

Step 5: Set the task and goal structure.

Step 6: Monitor the student-student interactions.

Step 7: Intervene to solve problems and teach skills.

Step 8: Evaluate the outcomes.

In addition, the research findings support changes in students' affect, such as:

- improved racial and ethnic relationships;
- increased self-esteem;
- more positive attitudes about school and subject matter;
- increased acceptance of differences, including of learners with special needs;
- increased group membership skills; and
- more frequent helping behaviors.

The procedures for forming cooperative learning groups consist of eight steps (see Table 8.1). These steps form the underlying structure for Sample Lesson 8.1. The lesson is a real example implemented in a fifth grade class to teach students literacy skills while reading a literature book. This example could be actualized in many different grade levels and across a variety of subjects.

Sample Lesson Using Cooperative Learning Groups

The design of the following lesson was a collaborative venture among four teachers as a part of their graduate studies: the classroom teacher, Chris Bretzke, and her colleagues, Evelyn Droeg, Teri Haugen, and Connie Rice. They took a graduate class with me where cooperative learning groups were used with adult learners. This lesson is an example of their group's application of cooperative learning in an inclusive classroom.

SAMPLE LESSON 8.1

Sample of a Cooperative Learning Group Lesson in a Fifth-Grade Classroom

In this project, a cooperative learning group structure was implemented in a fifth-grade classroom. This was an inclusive classroom with 24 students of various learning levels. The cooperative learning group method used was

Learning Together (see Table 8.2), where students work in small groups toward a single outcome after receiving instruction from the teacher.

◆ **Step 1: Determine the objective(s).**

1. To implement Learning Together in an inclusive classroom.

2. To teach students to complete a group project demonstrating literacy skills (i.e., reading, vocabulary words and definitions, writing, drawing, reading comprehension, and extension of learned concepts).

3. To read complete chapters in a literature book.

This lesson was a part of a literature study of the book *Tuck Everlasting*. The Learning Together procedure was used with 10 chapters of this book along with other learning procedures normally used in the classroom. In each of these 10 lessons, scheduled to occur on separate days, the students completed the assigned tasks cooperatively.

◆ **Step 2: Specify the group size and assign students to the groups.**

The classroom teacher decided to have six reading groups with four students in each group. The groups were formed with consideration given to ability, behavior, and personality. During the group's first meeting, members were asked to agree on a name for their reading groups. Group names and members were posted on the reading bulletin board.

It was also the responsibility of each group to divide fairly the reading and related activities among the group members. For example, some groups might decide to have each member take turns reading a paragraph while another group might decide to read half a page each to the end of the chapter. The groups also decided what the reading order of the members would be. The groups could change their reading order and the amount they read for each lesson.

◆ **Step 3: Arrange the classroom.**

Reading time occurred at 10:00 A.M. each morning for 1 hour. The students were instructed that they could complete their reading lesson by moving as a group to any part of the classroom they wanted to work. In choosing the location, the students had to be able to sit together in a circle with knees nearly touching. This was done so that, when they were reading aloud, whisper voices would be used and also to help them keep their focus.

Each day a different group member was responsible as a group leader and for completing the Group Record Form (see Appendix 8.A). This form asked the group leader to list group members' names, whether appropriate materials were brought to the group, whether the assignment was completed, and for comments about group participation and cooperation.

The Cooperative Learning Group Rules (see Table 8.3) were posted in the classroom. In the beginning, the teacher reviewed these rules with the large group, explaining each rule, asking questions, and giving examples of each rule. The students were reminded about these expected behaviors as needed as they worked in the cooperative learning groups.

◆ Step 4: Provide the appropriate materials.

For each cooperative learning group lesson, the students needed to bring their individual copies of the book and their individual dictionary, Group Record Forms, writing paper, drawing paper, and markers, as needed. The teacher provided the Group Record Forms and other necessary supplies by arranging those materials on a table for the group leader to pick up at the start of each lesson.

◆ Step 5: Set the task and group structure.

The teacher stated that the objectives of the lessons were to read the chapters assigned and do the activities in a fun way where the students could help each other. The students were told that reading in small groups would give them the opportunity to read orally more, which was something they enjoyed. It would give them an opportunity to share thoughts about the characters and story as well.

The students were then instructed to make positive comments on the Group Record Form and to include examples. Such an example might be that instead of writing "did not pay attention," it would be better to write the expected behavior, "should pay better attention." The students were reminded that each group member would take turns being the group leader and doing the Group Record Form. They were also reminded to keep comments directed to reading group participation.

The students were also told that each group would work at its own speed with a time limit given to all groups for completing the reading. If groups were not finished with the vocabulary words and writing exercises by that time, then the incomplete work would become individual homework or could be worked on as time permitted during the remainder of the day. Groups were also given hand-writing assignments that could be worked on if they were able to finish before reading time was over.

◆ Step 6: Monitor the student–student interaction.

The teacher monitored each group by walking around the classroom, observing, and listening as the groups completed their lesson. Praise was given, as warranted, to those who were participating appropriately.

The teacher also helped redirect or answer questions. Sometimes she took the opportunity to sit with a group and join in for a short time. At all times, the teacher was looking for positive comments, cooperative teamwork, and for the groups to be on task. The teacher also monitored student interactions by collecting the Group Record Forms daily and responding to comments. Additional monitoring occurred by teacher examination of the written work of the students and through the self-evaluation forms kept by each student in their literature journal.

◆ Step 7: Intervene to solve problems and teach skills.

The teacher intervened when a group or a student was having problems. If she heard something that was not positive, she would stop the group and redirect the students to the Cooperative Group Learning Rules. She would ask students to reflect on their actions to see how they did or did not apply those rules. If necessary, the teacher joined the group to model proper behavior and to refocus the group. After this, she would continue to monitor the group from a distance.

Most importantly, the teacher let the students know they had a choice to do their work together, in a more fun way with less work to do individually, or they could do all the assigned work individually. At the end of reading time, if all groups had done their job appropriately and had completed their assignments by pacing themselves and staying focused, they rewarded themselves by not having any reading homework.

◆ Step 8: Evaluate the outcomes.

The teachers who planned these lessons felt that the students and the classroom teacher had a wonderful experience (at least this is how they described it). According to them, there was a lot of growth in the areas of responsibility and cooperation. The students liked the structure and when given their assignment, they eagerly went to their groups and immediately began to work. The classroom teacher said, "It was a wonderful thing to see. Students who normally do not get excited about schoolwork followed along just like those students who love school."

There were aspects of Learning Together that this class continued to work on as they progressed through the lessons. One was keeping their voices to a whisper. Several times the class had to be stopped and reminded to lower their voices. The students did so, but after some time, the level would rise again. The teacher was pleased to see group members tap each other on the shoulder and give a signal to whisper. The teacher said that the students did try really hard and even though their voices would rise, for the most part, they were able to stay focused on reading.

The classroom teacher also said that as a class, it took little time to learn to write comments in a positive way. Occasionally, the teacher wrote examples on the board to give the students an idea of a positive comment. All Group Record Forms were saved from the beginning to the end, and great improvement could be seen. By the end of the lessons, nearly all comments were positive and very well done. For example, the following comments were included: "Excellent reading!" "Wonderful!" The team of teachers also said, "It is easy to get excited when you remember these comments were made by fifth-grade students about their peers. Never did a group have to be spoken to about inappropriate comments."

Some of the groups also had to work on pacing. Some groups paced themselves very well, watched the time, and finished when they should. Other groups were not as conscientious about the time and could get caught up in a discussion question, only to run out of time and have to complete the assignment as homework. (A remedy for this would be to assign a timekeeper.)

The teachers also thought that a part of learning to problem solve was learning to compromise, which was a big hurdle for the students. Groups had such questions as: Who would read first? How much does everyone read? How do you respond to certain behaviors? Some groups made these decisions easily from the very beginning. Other groups chose to spend a lot of the reading group time on these decisions at first and ended up doing their assignments as homework. It did not take long for these groups to make the choice to resolve these types of decisions easily so reading time could be spent on reading. The classroom teacher was rewarded to see the students make these transitions. As she walked around listening and observing, she would smile when she heard comments like, "Let's not waste anymore time. I don't want homework." "Come on, guys, let's just do it."

This project taught students self-awareness through group evaluation and self-evaluation. The classroom teacher said that the biggest lesson was that one could actually say something one did not like about someone in a positive way and in a way that would not hurt that person's feelings. She felt this was a real lesson in life.

In the self-evaluation, students had to look at themselves and think about whether they had done a good job. The teachers commented, "It is easy to look at other people and make judgments rather than it is to look at ourselves. Wow! The students were very honest with their opinions about themselves." One student wrote, "I could have worked harder." Another wrote, "Should have paid better attention."

The teachers observed that this way of learning was valuable for the poorer readers, as well as for the better readers. The poorer readers got the oral reading practice in a small, unthreatening environment. Readers could decide how much they would read. They could also follow along when the better readers read. They also gained comprehension from group discussions, as well as from sharing in the group's success. The better readers served as great reading models, served as peer tutors for those in the group who needed it, and were still able to progress through the book at a normal pace.

TABLE 8.2
Summary of Cooperative Learning Methods and Formats

---

1. Team-assisted individualization (TAI)

   TAI is a cooperative learning method in which heterogenous groups of students work to master individualized assignments (Slavin, Madden, & Stevens, 1990). Whereas other cooperative learning methods are group-paced, TAI is unique in that it combines cooperatively structured learning with individualized instruction. In TAI, individual group members work on their own assignments and assist other group members with their assignments. Group members are then rewarded if their team's performance meets or exceeds preestablished criteria.

2. Student teams achievement divisions (STAD)

   Students assemble in teams of four or five team members to master worksheets on material covered in a lesson just presented by the teacher. Subsequently, they individually take a quiz on that

---

(*continues*)

TABLE 8.2 *Continued.*

material. The team's overall score is determined by the extent to which each student improved over his or her past performance. The team demonstrating the greatest improvement is recognized in a weekly class newsletter. (Note: The descriptions of STAD, as well as the remaining four cooperative learning methods discussed below, are from Slavin (1981).)

3. Teams-games tournament (TGT)

The procedure in TGT is the same as that used in STAD, but instead of taking quizzes, the students play academic games with other members in the class whose poor performance was similar to their own. The team score is also based on individual improvement.

4. Jigsaw

Students meet in five- or six-member teams. The teacher gives each student an item of information that the student must "teach" to their team. Students are then individually tested for their mastery of the material. Jigsaw II is the same, except the students obtain their information from textbooks, narrative materials, short stories, or biographies. The class is then quizzed for individual and team scores.

5. Learning together

After the teacher has presented a lesson, students work together in small groups on a single worksheet. The team as a whole receives praise and recognition for mastering the worksheet.

6. Group investigation

This is a more complex method, requiring students to accept greater responsibility for deciding what they will learn, how they will organize themselves to master the material, and how they will communicate what they have learned to their classmates.

Note. From *Effective Instruction of Difficult-to-Teach Students: Instructor's Manual* (p. 151), by L. Idol and J. F. West, 1993, Austin, TX: PRO-ED. Copyright 1993 by PRO-ED. Reprinted with permission.

TABLE 8.3
Cooperative Learning Group Rules

1. Listen to others.
2. Encourage and respect others.
3. Explain and summarize.
4. Check for understanding.
5. Disagree in an agreeable way.

Several different learning methods and formats can be used with cooperative learning groups. Six commonly used ones are listed in Table 8.2. Each can be effective, but it is best for collaborating teachers to consider both the large group to be taught and the subject(s) to be taught. They should then reach consensus on the method that would be most suitable for that group. In Sample Lesson 8.1, the teachers decided to use the fifth method, Learning Together.

First, a class of students must be taught to learn in a cooperative structure. Once this very important piece is in place, then the multi-layered lesson is added, as described next.

Multi-Layered Lessons

Multi-layered lessons are those lessons that accommodate a range of student abilities and skills within a single lesson. This type of lesson is a good solution to classroom teachers' concerns that including students with special education needs has to result in such extensive curricular modifications that they would have to offer multiple lessons simultaneously. In the examples that follow, the teacher offers a single lesson for all students with a variety of learning activities and performance expectations embedded within the lesson.

Fundamental to the approach is the cooperative learning group structure. A sound set of instructional procedures is the second component of the multi-layered lesson. You will discover the elementary example of a multi-layered lesson is structured around the Basic Lesson Structure (see Appendix 8.B). This is simply one way of structuring such a lesson. Any sound set of instructional sequences could be used to form the base of the lesson. To further make this point, later in the chapter the example of a multi-layered lesson for a secondary class is structured around a different structure. This one is called a "model lesson plan," and is centered around teaching students to learn strategically and cognitively. Either structure could be used in either elementary or secondary classes.

The multi-layered lesson might take place in a single class session or it might extend over days, weeks, or months. It might be in a single subject area or within an integrated curriculum where two or more subjects are taught together. In the examples that follow, the elementary school example illustrates teaching long division with two inclusive classes and the secondary school example illustrates an integrated subjects application in a world history class.

A Multi-Layered Lesson in an Elementary Classroom

In this example of a multi-layered lesson, the lesson is centered around a Basic Lesson Structure (see Appendix 8.B) found to provide a reliable structure for students who are difficult to teach (see Idol & West, 1993). Thus, in Sample Lesson 8.2, the first instructional modification that was made was to use a highly structured lesson format for all students.

SAMPLE LESSON 8.2

Sample of a Multi-Layered Lesson in an Elementary Classroom

This multi-layered lesson was designed for two fourth-grade mathematics classes. Class A has 27 students and Class B has 26 students. In Class A there were three students with diagnosed learning disabilities, two with behavior problems, and two who were at risk for school failure. In Class B there was one student with learning disabilities, one with dyslexia and who read at a beginning level, three who were at risk for school failure, one who had severe behavior problems, and one who had cerebral palsy and used a wheelchair.

The two classrooms were adjacent to one another in a portable building in a K–4 school. For teaching mathematics, the two classroom teachers decided to teach math at the same time each day, working on the same lesson at the same time.

Support staff: In this school, there was an instructional assistant who was shared between these two teachers. During the time math was taught, the instructional assistant moved back and forth between the two classes, helping students who needed individual assistance.

In this school the single special education teacher worked primarily as a cooperative teacher, working in the classrooms with students. She worked primarily with special education students with IEPs, but also helped other students at times. In these two classes for math instruction, the cooperative teaching arrangement that was used was One Lead Teacher–One Support Teacher. The classroom teachers offered the primary lesson and the cooperative teacher served as a support teacher, working with individual students on an as-needed basis.

(Refer to Chapter 4 for further descriptions of this elementary school, which used cooperative teaching and instructional assistants.)

Basic Lesson Structure

◆ Step 1: Have a clear objective, often derived from a task analysis.

The objective of the lesson was to teach students to calculate long-division problems, following a specific sequence for completing the algorithm for division problems with a 2-place divisor and a 3-place dividend.

The steps in the algorithm were identified by the two classroom teachers and the cooperating teacher. They analyzed all of the subcomponents of solving a long-division problem and listing those subcomponents as steps. The steps are listed in Table 8.5.

◆ Step 2: Diagnose learners to make sure instruction is targeted at the correct level of difficulty.

Students were given a pretest on the basic math functions included in the algorithm for solving long-division problems. These included knowledge and mastery of place value, estimation, multiplication math facts, multiplication and subtraction with regrouping, remainders after subtraction, divisors, dividends, quotients, and whole numbers.

◆ Step 3: Gain learner's attention by focusing activities.

A large group discussion was held where the group brainstormed a list of all the instances in life where one would need to know how to calculate long-division problems.

◆ Step 4: Review relevant past learning.

Small group reviews were offered in any of the above listed knowledge areas for which a student might need clarification or reteaching. The groups were temporary review groups and group membership was based on performances on the pretest.

◆ **Step 5: Provide an "anticipatory set" by providing an overview, as well as the objective and purpose of the lesson.**

The objective of the lesson was presented to the students (see Step 1 above) by both classroom teachers to their respective classes. Each teacher went on to explain that the purpose for doing this lesson was so that every student would:

A. learn to use the step-by-step procedure for solving long-division problems.

B. learn to think aloud about what they are doing as they solve long-division problems.

C. learn to ask for assistance when they truly need it.

D. learn to check their own work.

E. learn to check their own understanding.

Both classroom teachers solved a demonstration long-division problem using an overhead projector and a large screen. They each explained to the students that they will all be learning to solve problems like this one and will be learning a step-by-step procedure that would be of great help to them. As they solved a second demonstration problem, they showed the students how they followed the 12 steps for completing a long division algorithm (see Table 8.4).

Both classroom teachers used a Model–Lead–Test teaching procedure, which is explained as follows and in Step 6.

Model—Both teachers worked a second long-division problem using the overhead projector. They displayed an overhead transparency of the 12 steps showing the students, each time, which steps they were on as the problem was solved.

◆ **Step 6: Provide information in small steps, with modeling and checking for understanding.**

Lead—Both teachers worked a third long-division problem, again using the overhead projector and the 12 steps. This time the students worked the same problem at their seats, following each step along with the teacher.

◆ **Step 7: Provide guided practice with immediate feedback and high success rates.**

Test—Each of the students then each worked a fourth long-division problem, following the 12 steps. Each classroom teacher then worked the same fourth problem on the overhead projector, so each student could compare their work to that of the teacher's, making any corrections that were needed.

◆ **Step 8: Provide opportunities for independent practice and reteaching, if necessary.**

The students then began working on a worksheet that had several long-division problems. The cooperative teacher, the instructional assistant, and the two classroom teachers then monitored the students, providing assistance and checking as the student progressed through the 12 steps.

Any students requiring reteaching were assigned to a temporary reteach group with the cooperative teacher.

◆ Step 9: Provide a final review of the lesson and an appropriate closure activity.

As a review of the lesson, students were assigned to small groups where each group was responsible for providing a humorous skit or demonstration to the class of how to work a long-division problem. All students then took a posttest. Students then returned to the small groups where they created more complicated types of long-division problems and presented them to the class.

TABLE 8.4
Steps for Completing a Long Division Algorithm

Step 1: Look at the divisor (number to the left of the half-box). Round to the nearest whole number in the tens column.

Step 2: Look at the dividend (number in the half-box). Round to the nearest whole number in the tens column.

Step 3: Estimate the approximate number of divisors in the dividend.

Step 4: Try this number in the tens place of the quotient (the number above the half-box).

Step 5: Multiply the estimated quotient (in tens place) times the divisor. Record this number in the hundreds and tens place underneath the dividend. Record a zero in the ones place underneath the dividend.

Step 6: Draw a line under this new number. Subtract this number from the dividend.

Step 7: Check to see if the remainder from the subtraction (Step 6) is less than the divisor. If it is, proceed to Step 8; if it is not, repeat Steps 1 to 6. If the number you got in Step 6 is more than twice the size of the divisor, use a larger estimated quotient. If the number you got in Step 6 is larger than the dividend and impossible to subtract from it, use a smaller estimated quotient.

Step 8: Repeat Steps 1 to 6 with the same divisor and the new dividend.

Step 9: Look at the remainder from the subtraction problem. If it is less than the divisor, record it after the quotient by writing the letter "r" and then this number. If it is more than the divisor, return to Steps 1 to 5 for the second estimation problem. Think about whether the incorrect answer to the subtraction problem was only one more value of the divisor or whether it was several times the value of the divisor.

Step 10: Check your work. Work the problem on the calculator. Did you get the same answer?

Step 11: (Extra Credit.) Skip Step 10 and calculate a multiplication problem to check your work. Clue: Multiply the divisor times the quotient you got and then add the remainder.

Step 12: Raise your hand to have an adult listen to how you solved this long-division problem.

TABLE 8.5

Modifications for Elementary Students with Special Education Challenges

Students with learning disabilities
1. worked every other problem on the worksheet on the calculator (if needed, to enhance attention and encourage work completion)
2. used a preprinted key of the multiplication tables (if needed)
3. were paired with a study buddy (if needed)

The student with dyslexia
1. used a preprinted key of the multiplication tables

The advanced students
1. worked at a faster pace
2. created story problems using the algorithm when their calculations were finished. This work could be done in teams or individually

The students who were at risk for school failure
1. were paired with a study buddy
2. used the preprinted key of the multiplication tables (if needed)

The student with physical challenges (cerebral palsy)
1. was paired with a study buddy
2. was provided with a larger worksheet with fewer problems and a bigger calculator

The students with behavior problems
1. were paired with two appropriately-behaving study buddies
2. had individualized contractual agreements with their teachers and parents for acceptable classroom behaviors
3. were given contractual points for good study behavior on a private basis by the classroom teacher

Sample Lesson 8.2 actually took place in the elementary school that is described in Chapter 5, in the sections under Cooperative Teaching and Instructional Assistants. In this real-life situation, two classroom teachers shared an instructional assistant. Because their classrooms were adjacent to one another, they decided to float the assistant across the two classrooms during math instruction.

These teachers also chose to have the cooperating teacher come into both classrooms simultaneously for the second half of the period each day. During the first half of the period, the teachers were involved in demonstration teaching. During the second half, the students were working independently and were given guided practice with the classroom teachers, the cooperating teacher, and the instructional assistant monitoring both classes. As described in the lesson, the cooperative teacher formed temporary small groups for any necessary re-teaching that was needed. She also closely monitored the work of the special education students.

Beyond the lesson, individual modifications were made for the various types of students. These modifications were used on an as-needed basis and are listed in Table 8.5, which shows IEP objectives for elementary students with learning challenges.

The need to create this lesson came from a real problem. With four adults working in two classes, it was discovered that each adult was using a slightly different explanation for how to work long-division problems. Thus, a multi-step procedure was developed that all adults and students would follow. This added a much-needed level of clarity to the instruction and guided practice sessions. For the first time, all students in both fourth grade classes learned to work long-division problems with mastery.

Also note that within the lesson, a direct instruction technique is used, referred to as a Model–Lead–Test teaching procedure. This is derived from the work of Englemann and Bruner (1974) and is replicated in many different forms in the works of Idol (1996a) and Idol and West (1993) as it applies to teaching students who are difficult to teach in inclusive situations.

Once a teaching structure has been embedded within the lesson, the multiple layers occur in the various modifications made for individual students who are still challenged by the learning situation.

A Multi-Layered Lesson in a Secondary Classroom

Sample Lesson 8.3 is a multi-layered lesson for a secondary classroom. It is designed to fit the Model Lesson Plan Form that can be found in Appendix 8.C. This Model Lesson Plan has been adapted from Lindquist (1987), and is as it appears in Idol and West (1993). Its focus is on teaching students how to be strategic learners and to develop critical thinking skills within the activities of the lesson.

This approach to teaching is centered around the use of cognitive instruction, which refers to any effort on the part of the teacher or the instructional materials to help students process information in meaningful ways and to become independent learners (Resnick, 1987). Resnick lists several efforts that contribute to this cognitively based approach to instruction:

1. Help students construct meaning from reading.
2. Teach students to solve problems.
3. Develop in students effective reading/thinking/learning strategies.
4. Teach students to select appropriate strategies.
5. Teach and expect students to take responsibility for their own learning.
6. Support students in transferring skills and concepts to new situations.

SAMPLE LESSON 8.3

Sample of a Multi-Layered Lesson in a Secondary Classroom

This multi-layered lesson was designed for a world history class of 25 students. Two of the students had diagnosed learning disabilities, four were at risk for school failure, one had moderate special education needs, and one had a hearing impairment.

For this lesson, the teacher divided the students into five groups of four students each and one group of five students. Each group formed a cooperative learning group, a structure which had been used previously in this class. The students with special needs were distributed across the groups as follows:

Group 1   two students, a student at risk, and the student with hearing
            impairment

Group 2   three students and the student with moderate special education needs

Group 3   three students and a student with learning disabilities

Group 4   three students and a student with learning disabilities

Group 5   three students and two students at risk for school failure

Group 6   three students and a student at risk for school failure (the one with the most serious problems)

Purpose of the Lesson: To compare Roman, Greek, and Indian empires

Time frame: 3 days

Preparation for Learning

◆ Assess Prior Knowledge

Students wrote or tape-recorded three brief essays on each of the three empires to be studied.

◆ Goals of the Lesson

1. To learn five dimensions for comparing cultures: time period, government, military, spiritual/religious/cultural practices, and economics.
2. To summarize knowledge about Roman, Greek, and Indian ancient empires.
3. To learn to make comparative timelines.
4. To learn to construct a matrix for making comparisons.

◆ Modifications of the Lesson

For special education students with IEPs, there were specific modifications that corresponded to their IEPs (see Table 8.6).

The teacher assigned the students to their respective groups and reminded them of the rules and procedures used in this class when working in a cooperative learning group.

Students filled in the matrix with any information they already knew about any of the three cultures to be studied (see Figure 8.1 for an example of a matrix). These were handed in to the teacher.

◆ Hints/Examples for Focusing

The teacher monitored pairs of students as they listed what they already knew in the matrix. She provided individual groups with hints and examples if they were struggling.

Presentation of Content

◆ Teacher Shows Examples and Nonexamples

The teacher demonstrated how the Roman Empire section in Figure 8.1 should look in the first row of the matrix. She showed examples of information from the textbook and resource materials that would fit the matrix and nonexamples that would not be applicable.

◆ Students Examine and Discuss Examples and Nonexamples

In the groups, students discussed why each of the examples and nonexamples provided by the teacher would or would not be fitted into the matrix.

◆ Small-Group Investigation

The students worked in the cooperative learning groups to gather more applicable information for the Roman Empire and all of the needed information for the Indian and Greek empires.

Pairs of students went to the school library or the computer lab to access World Wide Web information. They also gathered to do homework together (optional). This information was brought back to the cooperative learning group.

◆ Group Reports and Class Discussion with the Teacher

Each group's spokesperson reported to the class.
Each group made any necessary changes to their matrices based on the large group reports.

Integration and Application

◆ Graphic Organizers To Aid In Understanding

Student groups compared the contents of their matrices. They highlighted commonalities that were true for two empires with yellow highlighter and used blue highlighter for commonalities that were true for all three empires.

◆ Teacher Assesses Old Misconceptions

Individual students returned to their original prior knowledge matrix and constructed a new matrix.

Students returned to their cooperative learning groups, made a group list of misunderstandings, and then discussed their new understandings for each listed misconception.

Empires	Time Period	Government	Military	Spiritual/Religious/Cultural	Economics
Roman Empire					
Greek Empire					
Indian Empire					

Figure 8.1. Matrix for comparing empires.

◆ Additional

The entire class constructed a timeline comparing the three Empires and including the five dimensions of the completed matrices.

The teacher posed the question pertaining to our legacy from the past, "What aspects of each empire can be seen in American life today?"

The teacher posed a second legacy question, "What aspects of each empire can be seen in your own life today?"

Group and Individual Responsibilities

◆ Individuals

Every student in the class earned points for individual effort.

The student with hearing impairment had an interpreter.

The students with learning disabilities took responsibility for recording information on the graphs.

The student with moderate special education needs was required to:

- work on the team;
- find pictures from which the group could assimilate concepts onto the matrix;
- learn to work in a group with appropriate social behavior; and
- create symbols for use on the class timeline.

◆ Groups

Each group earned points for individual effort.

Each group was responsible for assigning these responsibilities:

- group recorder
- artist for the timeline
- readers of text
- selection of pictures
- interpretation of pictures

Pairs of students were assigned for gathering of resource information from textbooks and other resource materials.

Several aspects are essential to the success of this example of a multi-layered lesson. First, notice in the group structure that the types of students with challenges (learning disabilities, at risk for school failure, moderate special education needs, physical impairment) are distributed across the cooperative learning groups. This is so no one group is overburdened with students with challenges and so that each group is predominated by students who are experiencing normal or advanced school achievement.

Second, notice for the students with Individualized Education Programs (IEPs) that there are specific objectives for adaptations for them that tie back to their IEPs. Third, notice that students are assessed for group understandings, as well as for individual understandings. This is very important as some educators and parents are concerned that an adapted lesson using cooperative learning groups could result in

TABLE 8.6

Modifications for Secondary Students with Special Education Challenges

Students with learning disabilities
1. took the role of group recorder in cooperative learning groups to enhance understanding
2. learned to self-assess prior knowledge, as the teacher provided hints/examples for focusing
3. learned to develop graphic organizers and timelines to aid in understanding
4. learned to assess old misconceptions and misunderstandings

Student with moderate disabilities
1. learned to work on a team with appropriate social behavior
2. learned to find pictures to illustrate new information and understandings
3. learned to create and use symbols on a timeline to reflect understanding

Student with hearing impairment
1. was provided with an interpreter during class time and peer study time for world history class

individual students learning less. Fourth, notice that this is an example of an integrated curriculum. The students are studying world history, making application to modern life in America, using research skills, using a group communication process, using reading and writing skills, and doing group presentations.

Summary

The intent of this chapter has been to illustrate how an inclusive classroom can be designed to successfully accommodate a variety of types of learners, and yet offer each individual learner an opportunity for maximal growth and productivity. A progressive scaffold was presented that started first with use of cooperative learning groups. Then, added to this was a basic plan for instruction. Two examples were provided: a basic lesson structure often used with difficult-to-teach students and a model lesson plan centered around cognitive and strategic instruction. Finally, modifications and adaptations were added for individual students who had special learning or behavior challenges that prevented them from learning and producing in exactly the same way as other students in the inclusive class. As suggested in the title of this chapter, it is indeed possible for students to learn at different levels and rates in inclusive classrooms. The key is for teachers to teach students how to learn together and to use a multi-tiered structure to ensure that sound instruction is provided to all students.

APPENDIX 8.A
Group Record Form
I DID MY SHARE!

Name _____   Date _____

Group Name _____

Directions: Circle Always, Sometimes, or Never for each one.

I used a whisper voice	Always	Sometimes	Never
I was a good listener	Always	Sometimes	Never
I took turns	Always	Sometimes	Never
I had my materials	Always	Sometimes	Never
I followed directions	Always	Sometimes	Never
I did the best I could	Always	Sometimes	Never

Comments:

_____

_____

_____

_____

_____

_____

_____

© 2002 by PRO-ED, Inc.

APPENDIX 8.B
Basic Lesson Structure

1. Have a clear objective, often derived from a task analysis.

2. Diagnose learners to make sure instruction is targeted at the correct level of difficulty.

3. Gain learners' attention by focusing activities.

4. Review relevant past learning.

5. Provide an "anticipatory set" by providing an overview, as well as the objective and purpose of the lesson.

6. Provide information in small steps, with modeling and checking for understanding.

7. Provide guided practice with immediate feedback and high success rates.

8. Provide opportunities for independent practice and re-teaching, if necessary.

9. Provide a final review of the lesson and an appropriate closure activity.

Note. From *Effective Instruction of Difficult-To-Teach Students: Instructor's Manual* (p. vii), by L. Idol and J. F. West, 1993, Austin, TX: PRO-ED. Copyright 1993 by PRO-ED. Reprinted with permission.

APPENDIX 8.C
Model Lesson Plan Form

Preparation for Learning

1. Assess prior knowledge:

2. Goal of the lesson:

3. Activate prior knowledge:

4. Hints/examples for focusing:

Presentation of Content

1. Teacher shows examples and non-examples:

2. Students examine and discuss examples and non-examples:

3. Small-group investigations:

4. Group reports and class discussions with teacher:

Integration and Application

1. Graphic organizers are used to aid in understanding:

2. Teacher assesses old misconceptions:

Additional:

Students will be encouraged to monitor their own understanding by:

Note. From *Effective Instruction of Difficult-To-Teach Students* (p. 77), by L. Idol and J. F. West, 1993, Austin, TX: PRO-ED. Copyright 1993 by PRO-ED. Reprinted with permission.

CHAPTER NINE

◆ ◆ ◆ ◆ ◆ ◆ ◆ ◆ ◆ ◆ ◆ ◆ ◆ ◆ ◆ ◆ ◆ ◆

How Does One Become a Better Communicator?

◆ Although this chapter appears toward the end of this book, it is probably the most important chapter in guiding the development of collaborative and inclusive schools. Clear communication among individuals is the cornerstone of a truly civilized society, and must be in place if collaboration and inclusion are to evolve.

Our most precious resource is human relations. Through the shared intimacy of communication we can make sense of our lives, share them, and develop a stronger sense of community. We must be tolerant of differences of opinions, values, perspectives, and ideas as we work together to build a sense of community in our schools. And, we must model this tolerance for the students we teach if we are to influence how people work together in the future. One very influential way this tolerance is reflected is in how we do or do not listen to one another.

Active Listening

Six Basic Skills

Active listening is essential to the collaborative process, and collaborators are good listeners. They listen actively, meaning they are actively involved in the exchange. They use both verbal and nonverbal cues to let speakers know they are hearing and interested in what is being said. Verbally, they may use the six skills described below, say "u-hum" occasionally, or "go on," and so on. Nonverbally, they may nod their heads, look at the speaker, incline the head to one side, lean toward the speaker, or mirror the body position of the speaker.

Although there are many ways to describe the various communication skills, there are six particular skills that can form a strong base for effective communication. They are as follows: acknowledging, paraphrasing, reflecting, clarifying, elaborating, and summarizing (West, Idol, & Cannon, 1989). Table 9.1 contains definitions and examples of each of these six skills. Collaborative teams review these six skills, making certain they are aware of how to use each one. Teams can then practice using these skills in role-play sessions. My recommendation is that team members practice in groups of three with two people talking and one person observing. The speakers then select one or more skills they want to use consciously and keep this information to themselves.

TABLE 9.1
Definitions for Active Listening

1. *Acknowledging* involves indicating to speakers that you are listening to what is being said, that you are interested in what is being said, and that you are not judging what is being said.
   a. Nonverbal actions such as leaning toward speakers, maintaining eye contact, nodding, or showing appropriate facial expressions indicate an acknowledgment of the importance of communication.
   b. Responding to speakers with the same depth of feeling as they are using or responding in a manner that leads speakers to a slightly greater depth of feeling are most effective in conveying your acknowledgment of the intent of the conversation.
   c. Simple verbal responses such as, "I'm listening, please continue," "Yes," and "Right" facilitate the communication process.

2. *Paraphrasing* is an attempt on the part of listeners to feed back to speakers the essence of what they have just said using the listener's own words and expressions.
   a. Paraphrasing can convey to speakers that you are with them and are trying to understand what they are saying.
   b. Paraphrasing can crystalize people's comments by repeating what they have said in a more concise manner.
   c. Paraphrasing is a method for checking listeners' own perceptions to make sure they really do understand what speakers are describing.
   d. Paraphrasing entails some recognition of people's feelings from a cognitive or content perspective.

3. *Reflecting* is a response that focuses on speakers' feelings. Listeners share their perceptions of speakers' feelings and how they feel listening to speakers and/or how they would feel in a speaker's place.
   a. Reflecting the feeling being expressed is a skill that is appropriate at any time, regardless of the nature of the feeling (positive, ambivalent, negative) or the direction of the expression (toward self, toward others, toward the situation).
   b. A listener might say, "It sounds like this situation is very frustrating to you," in response to a speaker telling about the chaos that occurs in the classroom when one boy finishes his assignments early. With this type of reflecting response the speaker is free to agree, disagree, explain, etc.

4. *Clarifying* is a form of feedback in which listeners ascertain that the message sent is the message received.
   a. Some examples of clarifying are: "Is that about right?" "Do I understand your feelings correctly?" "Is this what you are saying?"
   b. Such clarifying responses are typically followed by a summary of what the speaker has conveyed, again clarifying to ascertain the accuracy of the message received.

5. *Elaborating* is a method of helping speakers move from less to more.
   a. For example, if speakers speak guardedly or are unclear about some issues, then listeners speak directly, clearly, and openly. What the speaker presents on a superficial level may be elaborated on by listeners at a more synthesized level.
   b. Elaborating may also be based on viewing the total communication of speakers, i.e., the verbal and nonverbal cues and the total meaning of these.

6. *Summarizing* is a method of pulling together the relevant data or information and letting it speak for itself. This technique is especially helpful when speakers have had trouble identifying the problem or have presented the information in a fragmented manner.
   a. When summarizing, use only information presented by speakers.
   b. When summarizing, select only the relevant data.

(continues)

TABLE 9.1 *Continued.*

c. Summarizing is a method of obtaining closure when speakers appear to have said everything they have to say but may not be certain that all has been said.

d. Summarizing can be a way for speakers to complete an information exchange, especially after it has been modeled by the listeners.

e. Summarizing should be used to give movement to the collaborative process, helping the communicators to move from one topic to another in an efficient and effective manner.

Note. From *Collaboration in the Schools: An Inservice and Preservice Curriculum for Teachers, Support Staff, and Administrators* (pp. 102–103), by J. F. West, L. Idol, and G. Cannon, 1989, Austin, TX: PRO-ED. Copyright 1989 by PRO-ED. Reprinted with permission.

After the simulated conversation, the observer can give both speakers feedback on what they observed in the exchange, including use of any of the six basic skills.

Much can be learned in this type of exchange. We are not always consciously aware of how we behave in communication exchanges. Soliciting observer feedback can be invaluable in finding out if others perceive us the way we perceive ourselves in our communications.

After the observer gives feedback, the triad rotates positions so that each team member has an opportunity to observe and give feedback, as well as to practice using the six essential skills. After the entire exchange, individual team members identify particular skills they want to continue to use more consciously in the team member meetings.

Communication

As well as being good listeners, effective collaborators understand the communication process. They know specific techniques and tools for enhancing their communication skills and model these skills when working with others. In this section, three areas pertaining to communication are reviewed: Ten Laws of Human Communication, some communication ideas, and some team communication skills.

Ten Laws of Human Communication

In addition to listening actively and perfecting the use of the six basic skills, collaborators are cognizant of what Hugh Mackay (1994), noted Australian social researcher, named the Ten Laws of Human Communication (see Table 9.2). Mackay has conducted participant-observation research in discussion groups of adults—adults purposefully assigned to groups by gender, age, race, culture, and education. By studying the various combinations of different types of groups, Mackay has reported that these 10 laws seem to be true regardless of individual differences among discussion groups.

Note that in the first law, Mackay emphasizes that it is not the message being sent that is the message, but rather the message that has been received. This is a basic tenet of good listening and collaboration. Often, we speak to others assuming that what we have said, or attempted to say, is what has been heard. In reality, though, the communication is what the listener has actually heard. That is why the six basic listening and

TABLE 9.2

Mackay's 10 Laws of Human Communication

1. It's not what our message does to the listener, but what the listener does with our message that determines our success as communicators.
2. Listeners generally interpret messages in ways that make them feel comfortable and secure.
3. When people's attitudes are attacked head-on, they are likely to defend those attitudes and, in the process, reinforce them.
4. People pay most attention to messages that are relevant to their own circumstances and point of view.
5. People who feel insecure in a relationship are unlikely to be good listeners.
6. People are more likely to listen to us if we also listen to them.
7. People are most likely to change in response to a combination of new experience and communication than in response to communication alone.
8. People are more likely to support a change that affects them if they are consulted before the change is made.
9. The message in what is said will be interpreted in the light of how, when, where, and who says it.
10. Lack of self-knowledge and an unwillingness to resolve our own internal conflicts make it harder for us to communicate with other people.

Note. Adapted from *Why Don't People Listen?* by H. Mackay, 1994, Sydney, Australia: Pan MacMillan.

responding skills are so essential to the communication act; so that listeners can give speakers feedback as to what has actually been received.

Communication Ideas

As exemplified in the work of Mackay (1994), communication is really an exchange of ideas and messages. Some of us were born into families where communications were clear and generally positive. Others of us come from families of origin where communication was garbled and often negative. Many of us come from families that fall somewhere between these two polar extremes.

But, regardless of our prior experiences with communication, we can learn to be better communicators. We can consciously use particular tools to aid us in creating communication exchanges that are reasonably comfortable, clear, and satisfying. This is an essential element of well-functioning collaborative teams.

Dyer and Dyer (1991), a wife–husband team who specialize in helping couples learn to improve their communications and relationships, have developed a list of 10 general ideas about effective communication. These ideas appear in adapted form for collaborators in Table 9.3. It is recommended that collaborators use these ideas in two ways. First, when forming a team, review the ideas and agree to practice them as a team. Second, when forming team or intrapersonal process goals (see Chapter 5), include any of these ideas in team goals.

Team Communication Skills

In addition to the use of active listening, the six basic skills, and adherence to Mackay's 10 Laws of Human Communication, there are also some basic ways of structuring problem-solving groups so effective communication is maximized. Four of them are discussed as follows.

TABLE 9.3
Communication Ideas

1. It is impossible not to communicate. Everything one says or does transmits information. If team members fail to greet one another when they come to the team meeting, they have communicated something to one another.

2. Communication takes two forms: verbal and nonverbal. Verbal communication occurs when messages are translated into words. Nonverbal communication relies on behavior.

3. Positive messages can and should be both verbal and nonverbal. Negative messages should always be verbal to avoid misunderstanding and to allow for discussion.

4. All communication occurs at two levels. The first level consists of the simple content of the message. For example, "I don't like this solution." The second level makes a statement about the team member's relationship with the other person. The style one uses in terms of tone of voice, timing, and other nonverbal factors conveys certain intentions toward the other person.

5. Totally open communication, i.e., conveying every thought one has, is disruptive to a relationship. All communication should be monitored. In caring relationships, positive messages significantly outnumber negative messages.

6. Negative feelings should not be ignored. Relationships are improved when negative messages are rephrased as positive, constructive requests for change.

7. The painful words and actions associated with negative messages are long remembered. Before expressing a negative message, ask yourself these three questions:

   A. "Is it true?"

   B. "Is it the right time?"

   C. "Is it constructive?"

   If the answer to any one of these questions is "No," the communication is likely to do more harm than good.

8. Focus your communication efforts on the future, not the past. The future can be changed.

9. Poor communication results from a lack of skills, not from a personality disorder. Communication skills can be learned. All new skills seem awkward in the beginning and this is certainly true of communication skills. Be patient and affirming with fellow collaborators.

10. Improved communication provides necessary tools for building a better relationship; but do not expect clear communication to make your collaborative team perfect. There are many other factors that go into building a successful collaboration.

Note. Adapted from *Growing Together: Couple Workbook* (2nd ed., pp. 11–12), by P. Dyer and G. Dyer, 1991, Minneapolis: Life Innovations.

Ball of yarn.   A ball of yarn is used to help groups achieve reciprocity in the group's conversations. In this case, reciprocity means that all members of the group have equal opportunities to share their ideas with the group. Sometimes groups experience difficulty because some members talk a lot and others talk very little or say nothing at all. Of course, some people are simply more talkative than others, but achieving a balance in contribution of ideas is important to developing a truly collaborative team process.

The ball of yarn is held by each group member when that person is talking. When the next person says something, the ball is passed to that person with the yarn trailing from the ball. As the conversation continues, the ball of yarn tracks a yarn trail from speaker to speaker. After a period of time, the group stops the team process and examines the pattern the thread of yarn has formed. The thread forms a very clear visual pattern of the balance or imbalance across the members of the group. Often, the visual pattern provides all the information that is needed for a group to move to a more reciprocal conversation exchange.

People will often modify their own behavior by simply examining the pattern formed by the thread. So, it is not necessary to repeat this exercise often. If the imbalance problem arises again, the exercise can be periodically repeated.

Communication whip. Another method to use to achieve group reciprocity in conversations is communication whip. If the ball of yarn does not alter the group's behavior immediately, the communication whip can provide a structure that will control the problem.

With communication whip, each member of the group takes a turn in offering ideas to the group. This strategy is particularly helpful during the brainstorming part of the problem-solving process discussed in Chapter 5. The turn taking occurs by each member taking their turn as the turns rotate around the group. If a member is not ready to speak when their turn arises, they say "Pass." Group members are encouraged to limit their words by trying to say their expressions concisely and directly. Communication whip controls for both the over-talkative person and the one who never speaks.

Finger signals. Use of finger signals is another effective way for the group to move more quickly through the problem-solving process. Finger signals facilitate the process because a message can be sent quickly with the fingers without having to use so much time for verbal expressions. Some examples of how they can be used follow.

Finger signals can be used to indicate that time is running out without the timekeeper having to speak. The timekeeper can simply point to the clock. They can be used to indicate that it is time to stop or move on to another topic by drawing the index finger across the throat, the same signal used by water-skiers to signal the driver of the boat to stop.

Finger signals can also be used to facilitate the decision-making process. For example, a team can quickly decide whether an issue has been resolved. At any point in the meeting, any member can call for a signal from all team members, indicating whether the issue has been resolved for each individual. At the point the signal call is made, all team members hit their right fist in their left palm two times, and then on the third time they extend their right hands to the center of the table (or group configuration) with the right hand either in a closed fist or with an open, extended palm. The closed fist indicates the issue is resolved for that member; an open palm means that more discussion is needed. One or more open palms means the group will further their discussion. All closed fists means the group is ready to move to the next issue or close the meeting, whichever is the case.

TABLE 9.4

SLANTing in Collaborative Teams

S = Sit up straight, looking professional and interested in what is being said.
L = Lean toward the person who is speaking.
A = Act interested and ask relevant and pertinent questions.
N = Nod your head occasionally as the speaker is talking.
T = Track the speaker; follow the speaker with your eyes.

Each collaborative team is encouraged to develop their own unique nonverbal signals that might facilitate their team process or their communication exchanges. Doing this can contribute to team members building their own personal group identity; plus it can add a sense of spirited fun to the team process.

SLANTing. Cecil Mercer, through work at the Kansas Institute for Research on Adolescents with Learning Disabilities at the University of Kansas, developed a strategy called SLANTing in the Classroom. The original strategy was developed to teach students a proper way of behaving in a classroom. I have adapted the SLANT strategy to use with collaborative teams, which is displayed in Table 9.4. A SLANTing team is impressive to watch. They look good! They look interested, professional, and on task. They appear to be treating one another with respect and interest, which is reflected, at least on the exterior, by their SLANTing behavior. At a bare minimum, it is recommended that all beginning collaborative teams use SLANTing as it has been adapted. SLANTing provides a physical structure that allows the group a solid place from which to begin their collaborative work.

Principles of Collaborative Consultation

In the Collaborative Consultation Model developed by my colleagues and I (Idol, Nevin, & Paolucci-Whitcomb, 1994), we have identified several different principles of collaborative consultation that we have found to be helpful in developing collaborative partnerships. We learned them from observing many teachers as they were preparing to be consulting teachers. These are displayed in Table 2.2 in Chapter 2, Principles of Collaborative Consultation. It is recommended that each team member adhere to these principles, actively practicing them and demonstrating their application during the team meetings.

If a team starts to have problems, the first thing to do is for individual members to review the contents of Table 2.2 in Chapter 2 and determine if any of those principles are being violated. Then, if an individual finds one or more principles that need to be improved, it is recommended that this improvement challenge be done first privately by individuals. The areas needing improvement can be targeted as interpersonal goals to be worked on and privately monitored (see Chapter 5 for a description of the collaborative problem-solving process, which includes the setting of private, intrapersonal goals).

After individuals have checked and monitored their private behavior, the team checks on its behavior as a group. First, the team refers back to the group process goal(s) set during the initiation of the problem-solving process. Discussion and assessment of progress might be followed by modifying existing goals or setting new goals.

Self-Assessment of Communication Skills

Another way to monitor one's own behavior in the collaborative team process is to periodically assess one's use of the various communication skills. Appendix 9.A contains an assessment instrument to be used for this purpose. It can be used either privately by individuals, as with the Principles of Collaborative Consultation, or by the entire team.

Examination of the Team Process

Finally, periodically the entire team should stop its team process and examine how well the process itself is functioning. Appendix 9.B is an instrument for teams to use for this purpose. Again, refer back to Chapter 3, where the stages of problem solving are explained. Note that during the goal-setting stage, the team is expected to have at least one simple way of monitoring the team process. In identifying which process skills to work on, some of the items from this instrument may be ones the team will need to target for improvement.

Appendix 9.B could also be used by individuals as a means of improving their own intrapersonal behaviors. If the items are used in this way, it is recommended that they be worked on privately.

Summary

A team that communicates well is one that has built a very strong foundation for conducting collaborative problem solving. In this chapter, you have read about strategies for improving your listening skills, intrapersonal and team communication skills, nonverbal skills, and the ways in which you treat and interact with your teammates. The various assessment instruments and checklists can help you and your team as you endeavor to become collaborators and team players.

APPENDIX 9.A
Self-Assessment of Communication Skills

1. Are you a good listener? _____

2. Do others say you are a good listener? _____

3. Do you make hurrying noises and gestures when others are talking that indicate you are not listening? _____

4. Are your thoughts racing ahead of the speaker's words? _____

5. Are you actively practicing the six basic listening and responding skills:

   _____ Acknowledging?   _____ Paraphrasing?

   _____ Reflecting?   _____ Clarifying?

   _____ Elaborating?   _____ Summarizing?

6. Are there any of these six basic skills you need to improve? Which one(s)? _____
   _____

7. Have you recently reviewed the 10 Laws of Human Communication? Which ones do you need to remind yourself of? _____
   _____

8. Do you ask one question at a time? And then wait for the response? _____

9. Is there consistency between what you communicate verbally and nonverbally? _____

10. Do you send one clearly received message at a time? _____

11. Do you prevent your biases or preconceived ideas from interfering with your listening? _____

12. Do you wait for the speaker to complete a message rather than interrupting to express your own ideas? _____
    _____

© 2002 by PRO-ED, Inc.

APPENDIX 9.B
Examination of the Team Process

Self   Group

_____ _____ 1. There is a designated meeting time that works for all team members.

_____ _____ 2. The time allocation for our meetings is of sufficient duration.

_____ _____ 3. Our group size is 5–7 members.

_____ _____ 4. We use a problem-solving worksheet that aids us in our process and documents our team efforts.

_____ _____ 5. We have a parity-based team where all members are treated equally.

_____ _____ 6. We stop occasionally to examine our group process.

_____ _____ 7. We are always working to improve a team process skill.

_____ _____ 8. We take responsibility for beginning and ending meetings on time.

_____ _____ 9. We encourage multiple perspectives and understandings of the problem to be solved.

_____ _____ 10. We actively consider a number of different solutions to the problem.

_____ _____ 11. We carefully analyze the pros and cons for the various possible solutions.

_____ _____ 12. We reach consensus on the best solution to the problem.

_____ _____ 13. We implement one solution at a time.

_____ _____ 14. We develop a Plan of Action that lists the necessary details for implementing the solution.

_____ _____ 15. We continuously evaluate our group process.

_____ _____ 16. We monitor and evaluate our progress toward solving the problem.

_____ _____ 17. When evaluating, we use simple methods that are easy to implement in inclusive classrooms.

_____ _____ 18. The entire team agrees before we release to others any information we have gathered.

_____ _____ 19. We use Communication Whip when we have trouble with equitable sharing of ideas.

_____ _____ 20. We have comradery within our team.

_____ _____ 21. Occasionally, we invite an observer to watch our team process and give us feedback.

_____ _____ 22. We give feedback to one another on our group process skills.

_____ _____ 23. We receive feedback graciously and in the spirit of wanting to improve our communication and team interaction skills.

_____ _____ 24. We consciously use SLANTing during our group meetings.

© 2002 by PRO-ED, Inc.

CHAPTER TEN

◆ ◆ ◆ ◆ ◆ ◆ ◆ ◆ ◆ ◆ ◆ ◆ ◆ ◆ ◆ ◆ ◆

What Can Be Done To Support Changes in Attitudes and Beliefs?

◆ A hard reality in building collaborative and inclusive schools is that not everyone in a school wants to do this. Building collaborative and inclusive schools requires two major conceptual shifts for some people who are simply not prepared to face such changes.

One conceptual shift, pertaining to collaboration, is that some teachers are accustomed to teaching in isolation, away from other professional adults. They are not accustomed to working in teams, teaching in teams, or making group decisions. They are accustomed to working alone and making unilateral decisions. Being caught in a school-wide movement toward collaboration can be threatening to such individuals.

A second conceptual shift, pertaining to inclusion, is that some teachers are very comfortable in the way things have always been done regarding special education. They are accustomed to and prefer to make a referral to special education for a student who is difficult to teach or manage. They often expect this referral will result in a special education placement, with such a placement typically involving removal of the student from the general classroom to a special education classroom. More than half the time, placement decisions such as these result in the student remaining in the general education classroom for half or more of the school day. Yet, some teachers cling rather tenaciously to the belief that somehow the student with special needs will be removed from their classrooms.

What Is Needed?

Change is needed in attitudes and beliefs about how students best learn. Change is inevitable. Change is ongoing. Life is not stagnant. Life in schools is certainly not stagnant. The key is to support staff in accepting change and learning to embrace change.

Facing Fears

People are resistive, especially to change, when they feel threatened. Sometimes the threat may be real; sometimes it may be imagined. Regardless of which source it is, fears are best handled when they are faced. Faculty should be encouraged and supported in identifying their fears about developing collaborative and inclusive schools. These fears, when appropriate and legitimate, should be shared with the entire faculty so the entire group can engage in collaborative problem solving.

Planning a Proactive Vision

In a collaborative school, a faculty comes together to identify both real and potential problems and to generate solutions to those problems. The primary objective for this group gathering is to create a vision of what the collaborative and inclusive school will look like. The creation of this vision should be done by supporting the entire group in reaching consensus on that vision. The consensus-building process is based on the premise that the entire group will create a vision that all faculty members can "live with," morally and professionally.

The vision creation is done in a proactive manner, rather than a reactive one. The focus is placed on creating the vision in advance of implementation rather than creating a vision that is reactive to particular interest groups or problems. It is vitally important to the group's mental health and synergy that emphasis be placed on taking a positive, proactive stance in creating this vision.

Supporting the Faculty

In my experiences as a school consultant, the biggest shifts in alleviating resistance occur when a faculty feels supported. The most important source of support comes from the principal. Job satisfaction, willingness to take risks, and embracing challenges and changes occur in schools where the teachers feel the principal is behind them and supporting them.

The most resistive faculty may feel that the principal should support the status quo—keeping things as they have always been. The faculty may need guidance and coaching to see that positive support can come in more future-oriented forms such as faculty staff-development opportunities; provision of professional time for collaboration; creation of a school-wide vision; development of concrete ways of supporting an inclusive classroom (as discussed in Chapter 4); and the fostering of more successful classroom experiences for students. By providing such support and opportunities, the principal may be instrumental in helping the most resistive faculty appreciate the positive outcomes that can be achieved in the course of implementing planned change.

Providing Systematic Staff Development

One of the most effective methods of supporting teachers and in bringing about change is through staff development. The content of this effort should be carefully planned using the conceptualizations in the various chapters in this book as a guide.

In building collaborative and inclusive schools, staff members typically need development opportunities in two primary areas: (a) how to work together and (b) what to do in the inclusive classrooms. A more detailed listing of suggested areas for staff development is as follows:

- the collaborative problem-solving process;
- refinement of team collaboration and communication skills;
- methods of effective assessment, instruction, and student evaluation in inclusive classrooms;
- development of the various school-wide vehicles for collaboration (see Chapter 4);
- development of various ways of supporting classroom teachers in inclusion (see Chapter 4);
- further development of learning to manage conflict and confrontation;
- process and outcome evaluation;
- coaching in the inclusive classrooms.

Providing a Forum for Concerns

Each faculty, with its principal, needs to establish a forum for how concerns will be communicated and shared. This forum might be periodic faculty meetings with specific time devoted to raising concerns and exploring solutions. Another would be to establish a policy where a concerned individual might leave e-mail or personal messages with specific individuals, such as the principal, assistant principals, department representatives, grade level team chairpersons, inclusion coordinators, and so on. If site-based management is to be used, establishing a way for individual concerns to be brought to this team would be appropriate. There are several ways this could be done; what matters is that at least one consistent forum for expression of concerns be established.

Redefining and Clarifying Roles and Responsibilities

One of the primary reasons why faculty can be resistive is that they sometimes have personal concerns about job security. They fear the change because if too much change occurs, their skills might be obsolete for their professional position. Aside from staff development, it is vital for all concerned in the collaborative and inclusive effort to be certain of what is expected of them and of others with whom they will be working. (See Chapter 4 for a more in-depth discussion and examples of job descriptions, roles, and responsibilities.) Clarification of what will be expected of all professionals involved and having the entire group determine those expectations will greatly assist in alleviating concerns about job security.

Evaluating Change

Knowing in advance how change will be evaluated is a vital part of creating the collective vision of collaborative and inclusive schools. Unfortunately, many school faculties wait until the change has been implemented to explore how to document changes. Taking a proactive stance is essential to evaluation.

Change in collaborative and inclusive schools can be evaluated in three different dimensions: (a) changes in students, (b) changes in the adults involved, and (c) changes within the schooling system itself. Examples of types of change to evaluate in each of these three areas are listed in Table 10.1.

TABLE 10.1
Three Dimensions of Evaluating Change

Student Change

- Academic Skills/Grades
- Attitudes
- Social Behaviors

Team Change

- Skills in the Knowledge Base
- Interpersonal and Communication Skills
- Intrapersonal Attitudes and Beliefs

System Change

- Classroom
- Building
- District

Accepting and Managing Resistance Effectively

Aside from the above-discussed areas, resistance itself is a formidable force that must be identified and accepted. Acceptance can then result in choosing to use specific strategies to manage resistance and to support people in making both institutional and individual changes.

Managing Institutional Resistance

Figure 10.1 is a very useful guide in understanding how to bring about change successfully within an organization. The small circle in the middle illustrates how small individuals within an organization might feel as they experience change being forced upon them (illustrated by the larger circle).

Surrounding the smaller circle are seven variables that influence how the change is perceived and received by the individuals in the organization. The fewer the number of variables in place within the organization, the smaller the inner circle. This represents how individuals might feel very small and unimportant within the organization. As this smaller circle tightens, it illustrates how the individuals become smaller, tighter, and more resistive.

When the seven variables are all in place, the small inner circle begins to expand. This illustrates how individuals, when properly supported, become more established and realize more fully that they comprise the organization.

An important step toward recognizing and accepting resistance is to use this figure to better understand how empowered and expansive the individuals within your school feel. Asking these questions is helpful to this process:

- Do you all have seven variables in place?
- Does the entire faculty perceive them to be in place?
- Are all seven working?
- Are they accessible to each and every one of the faculty and staff?

If this is the case, the resistance in your school is probably minimal and your faculty are empowered to work together and to own and celebrate the changes they are

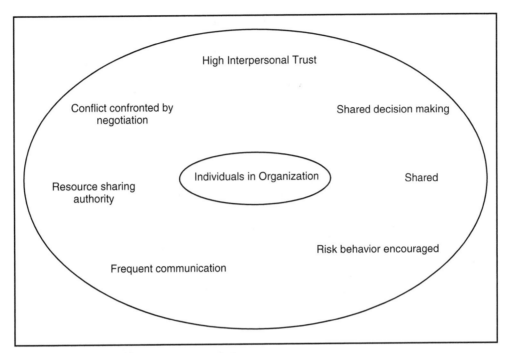

Figure 10.1 Facilitating organizational change.

building. If it is not the case, identify those areas that are problematic. Then, develop a collaborative plan to ensure that each of the seven variables is put into place.

An additional approach to managing institutional resistance is to apply specific strategies for dealing with resistance to change. There are 16 such strategies listed in Table 10.2, as offered by Pokras (1989). Change agents should refer to this list often to ensure they are making progress using each of the 16 strategies.

Managing Individual Resistance

The primary base for managing resistance is to build support at the building level, as described above. However, certain individuals within your school may be highly resistive—resistive enough to cause difficulties that go beyond that individual. It is important to recognize that negative behavior can be contagious, especially if negators also feel they are being victimized. Others on the faculty will get caught up in the negative and resistive movement. Often when this type of escalation occurs, truths get a little distorted, fears get heightened, and trust erodes quickly.

It is important to provide a forum for all faculty to come together to explore and share their attitudes and beliefs about the change. This heterogenous mix is important because negators have difficulty seeing the positive benefits and aspects of a change. Being exposed to others who have a more positive view is helpful in supporting the resistors to change.

In my experience, the forum for sharing of attitudes and beliefs is best accomplished through a staff development session. The time should be divided into three different phases of introspection.

Phase one. The first phase should be a time for individuals to process information and examine their attitudes and beliefs in a private and protected manner. For example, you

TABLE 10.2

Strategies for Managing Resistance to Change

1. Accept it.
2. Empathize.
3. Know before you go.
4. Analyze the consequences.
5. Involve staff.
6. Give advanced warning.
7. Beat the grapevine.
8. Present it positively.
9. Vent resistance.
10. Stress benefits.
11. Explain the purpose.
12. Reassure them.
13. Stress growth and development.
14. Include systematic training.
15. Change gradually.
16. Recognize and reinforce supporters.

Note. Adapted from *Systematic Problem Solving and Decision Making,* by S. Pokras, 1989, Los Altos, CA: Crisp.

might show a faculty group a short film of students with disabilities being integrated in general education programs. Immediately after the viewing, the individuals examine their own private thoughts and beliefs, being reminded to be kind to themselves and to allow themselves to experience any thought or belief that appears for them, rather than shutting off such feelings with shame, guilt, denial, projection, anger, and so. An effective way for people to do this self-examination is for them to write down their feelings without censorship or editing. These writings are totally private and should never be read by others.

Phase two. In the second phase, individuals are encouraged to share the feelings and ideas they want to with the two individuals seated most closely to them. This could be for about 10 minutes.

Phase three. In the third phase, the group leader brings the entire group together to share any impressions, ideas, and beliefs they feel the entire group would benefit from hearing. The entire group is reminded that all will practice nonjudgmental responding, accepting that all that is shared has come from within the group and exists whether or not it is shared with others.

Recognizing barriers. After this, the third phase is extended even further. The entire group is divided into small groups of three to five people on a random basis. This is important so that the small groups consist of rich blends of various types of individuals who may not voluntarily work or sit together. Each small group then generates a list of possible barriers to implementing the change. These ideas are brainstormed and listed nonjudgmentally, treating all ideas as being equally valid. This process takes about 10 minutes. Each small group has a timekeeper, a recorder, and a team spokesperson.

The group leader then brings the entire group back together and asks the small-group spokespersons to share their list with the large group. These barriers are listed on large sheets of paper by one or two large group recorders. It can be a useful strategy to ask negators to help with the recording process, thus getting them more directly involved with the group process. As each idea is listed, each of the other small group spokespersons raises their hand if the barrier reported is also on their list. Another person counts the hands and announces the count to the group recorder, who writes the number by the barrier reported on the large sheet. The other team spokespersons eliminate any of these items from the list they will read to the large group.

Creating solutions. The group then returns to the smaller groups, where each group selects the three worst barriers from the group master list of barriers. They generate at least three solutions for each of the three barriers. These are then reported back to the large group. These solutions are then typed and disseminated to the entire group for further individual thought. Finally, at a final meeting the entire faculty endorses at least one solution or more for each barrier that was perceived by many to be an obstacle.

This process works very well and gets everyone involved in the decision making. It helps a faculty reach consensus more easily on how to solve the major obstacles and empowers them to get involved in solution resolution, not just barrier identification. The large group sharing process also helps people who have ideas that are much more negative than the rest of the group to obtain a broader and more positive perspective.

Resolving Conflict Peacefully

Many people fear conflict. This fear causes us to gravitate toward people who think like us and who agree on the issues. Sometimes people have a distorted sense of fear because they were reared in families where conflict resulted in disasters. They sometimes mistakenly fear that *any* conflict or disagreement will result in disaster, which very rarely happens among professionals. The first step in conflict resolution is to help people to see that disagreement can be very healthy, because it lends itself to empowerment, as one finds oneself managing these difficult behaviors by applying specific strategies that do much to nullify and pacify trying situations. Table 10.3 provides a list of peaceful conflict resolutions, and Table 10.4 offers strategies for identifying and managing difficult people.

TABLE 10.3

Peaceful Conflict Resolution

Respect the rights of others.
Express your concerns.
Share common goals and interests.
Open yourself to different points of view.
Listen carefully to all proposals.
Understand the major issues involved.
Think about probable consequences.
Imagine several possible alternative solutions.
Offer some reasonable compromise.
Negotiate mutually fair, cooperative agreements.

TABLE 10.4
Strategies for Identifying and Managing Difficult People

Personality type	Characteristics	Strategies
Attackers	hostile, aggressive, abusive, intimidating	• let them blow off steam and express their anger • do not let them run on; say their name: "David, I hear what you are saying. Let's sit down and talk about it." • take what they say seriously; hear them and let them know you hear them and then state your position clearly • avoid the temptation to argue
Egotists	experts, often know more than others; love to show off; others frustrate them	• let them speak first, allowing time for them to "bask in their knowledge" • be prepared with the facts, because you cannot "fake it" with egotists
Sneaks	take potshots, undercut authority in devious ways by using sarcasm, often disguised as a joke	• never ignore their snide comments; instead, expose them • when they snipe, be direct and ask them for their opinions and solutions • force them into the open and you weaken their ability to cause problems
Victims	see everything negatively; they complain, whine, seem to be powerless, and act defeated	• since they often believe no one thinks they are important, take them seriously • start your interactions by listening to what they have to say • steer them toward the facts, which are usually less negative than their interpretations • maintain control by bringing up the negatives yourself and then dismiss each logically • direct their attention to the more positive aspects of a situation
Negators	are not just negative, they distrust anyone in power, and believe their way is the only right way; favorite motto: "I told you so."	• stay positive, but realistic • delay discussion of solutions since they will dismiss any solution as soon as others bring it up • wait until solutions start to come from them • refuse to argue with them and stick to the facts • anticipate objections they may raise and prepare facts and information to refute them

(continues)

TABLE 10.4 *Continued.*

Personality type	Characteristics	Strategies
Superagreeable people	easy to like; a very difficult type; outgoing and friendly; strong need to be liked; become whatever others need them to be at their own expense; terrified of making mistakes; cannot say "No" and overcommit themselves	• it is hard to discover the truth because they say what they think others want to hear • listen carefully to what they have to say when their guard is down • listen to their humor, which often reveals their true value systems • carefully limit how much you ask of them, to eliminate their own disappointments by missed and delayed deadlines • teach them about realistic workloads • help them to see things in proper perspective
Unresponsive people	human "clams" of society; most difficult to deal with; do not reveal their true motives; hard to understand; difficult to draw out	• the most effective strategy is to draw them out • always ask them open-ended questions that require more than "yes/no" answers • give them time to respond even if there is a long period of silence • if they refuse to respond, agree to meet again later and ask them to think about specific topics you will discuss at that time

Note. Adapted from "Managing Difficult People," by M. Manning and P. A. Haddock, 1988, November, *Sky Magazine*, p. 128, 132–134.

Summary

In this chapter we have explored one of the more challenging aspects of building collaborative and inclusive schools—learning to accept and manage resistive behavior. We have examined some basics that are needed in all situations, and then moved to exploration of specific strategies for managing resistance in organizations as well as resistance in particular individuals.

REFERENCES

American Association of School Administrators, National Association of Elementary School Principals, and National Association of Secondary School Principals. (1988). School-based management: A strategy for better learning. Arlington, VA: Author (AASA); Alexandria, VA: Author (NAESP); Reston, VA: Author (NASSP).

Bauwens, J., & Hourcade, J. J. (1995). Cooperative teaching: Rebuilding the schoolhouse for all students. Austin, TX: PRO-ED.

Bauwens, J., Hourcade, J. J., & Friend, M. (1989). Cooperative teaching: A model for general and special education integration. Remedial and Special Education, 10(2), 17–22.

Brookover, W., Beady, D., Flood, P., Schweitzer, J., & Wisenbaker, J. (1979). School social systems and student achievement schools can make a difference. New York: Praeger.

Canter, L., & Canter, M. (1982). Assertive discipline: A take charge approach for today's education. Los Angeles: Lee Canter and Associates.

Chalfant, J. C., & Van Dusen Pysh, M. (1989). Teacher assistance teams: Five descriptive studies on 96 teams. Remedial and Special Education, 10(6), 49–58.

Duckett, W., Parke, D., Clark, D., McCarthy, M., Lotto, L., Gregory, L., Herling, J., & Burlson, D. (1980). Why do some schools succeed? The Phi Delta Kappan study of exceptional elementary schools. Bloomington, IN: Phi Delta Kappa.

Dyer, P., & Dyer, G. (1991). Growing together: Couple workbook (2nd ed.). Minneapolis: Life Innovations.

Edmonds, R. (1979). Effective schools for the urban poor. Educational Leadership, 37, 15–24.

Education for All Handicapped Children Act of 1975, 20 U.S.C. § 1400 et seq.

Englemann, S., & Bruner, E. C. (1974). DISTAR: An instructional system—Reading 1. Chicago: Science Research Associates.

Fagen, S. A. (1986). Least intensive interventions for classroom behavior problems. The Pointer, 31(1), 21–28.

Fuchs, D., & Fuchs, L. S. (1994). Inclusive schools movement and the radicalization of special education reform. Exceptional Children, 60(4), 294–309.

Gardner, H. (1993). Multiple intelligence: The theory in practice. New York: Basic Books.

Glasser, W. (1977, November–December). Ten steps to good discipline. Today's Education, 61–63.

Hord, S. M. (1986). A synthesis of research on organizational collaboration. Educational Leadership, 44, 22–26.

Idol, L. (1989). The resource/consulting teacher: An integrated model of service delivery. Remedial and Special Education, 10(6), 38–48.

Idol, L. (1990). The scientific art of classroom consultation. Journal of Educational and Psychological Consultation, 1(1), 3–22.

Idol, L. (1993). Special educator's consultation handbook (2nd ed.). Austin, TX: PRO-ED.

Idol, L. (1994a). Don't forget the teachers. The Journal of Emotional and Behavioral Problems, 3(3), 28–33.

Idol, L. (1994b). Key questions related to inclusion and collaboration in the schools. The Consulting Edge, 6(1), 1–3.

Idol, L. (1996). Collaborative consultation and collaboration. In J. Lupart, A. McKeough, & C. Yewchuk (Eds.), Schools in transition: Rethinking regular and special education (pp. 22–241). Toronto: Nelson-Canada.

Idol, L. (1997a). Key questions related to building collaborative and inclusive schools. Journal of Learning Disabilities, 30(4), 384–394.

Idol, L. (1997b). Reading success: A specialized literacy program for students with challenging reading needs. Austin, TX: PRO-ED.

Idol, L., Nevin, A., & Paolucci-Whitcomb, P. (1994). Collaborative consultation (2nd ed.). Austin, TX: PRO-ED.

Idol, L., Paolucci-Whitcomb, P., & Nevin, A. (1986). Collaborative consultation. Austin, TX: PRO-ED.

Idol, L., & West, J. F. (1989). Collaboration in the schools: The problem-solving process [Video]. Austin, TX: PRO-ED.

Idol, L., & West, J. F. (1991). Educational collaboration: A catalyst for effective schooling. Intervention in School and Clinic, 27(2), 70–78, 125.

Idol, L., & West, J. F. (1993). Effective instruction of difficult-to-teach students: An inservice and preservice professional development program for classroom, remedial, and special education teachers. Austin, TX: PRO-ED.

Idol, L., West, J. F., & Lloyd, S. (1988). Organizing and implementing specialized reading programs: A collaborative approach involving classroom, remedial and special education teachers. Remedial and Special Education, 9(2), 54–61.

Idol-Maestas, L., & Ritter, S. (1985). A follow-up study of resource/consulting teachers. Teacher Education and Special Education, 8(3), 121–131.

Individuals with Disabilities Education Act of 1990, 20 U.S.C § 1400 *et seq.*

Johnson, D. W., & Johnson, R. T. (1987). *Learning together and alone: Cooperation, competition, and individualization.* Englewood Cliffs, NJ: Prentice Hall.

Johnson, D. W., Maruyama, G., Johnson, R., Nelson, D., & Skon, L. (1981). Effects of cooperative, competitive, and individualistic goal structures on achievement: A meta-analysis. *Psychological Bulletin, 89*(1), 47–62.

Kauffman, J. M., & Hallahan, D. P. (1995). *The illusion of full inclusion: A comprehensive critique of a current special education bandwagon.* Austin, TX: PRO-ED.

Kubick, K. (1988). *School-based management* (ERIC Digest Series). Eugene, OR: ERIC Clearinghouse on Educational Management.

Lewis, R. B., & Doorlag, D. H. (1991). *Teaching special students in the mainstream* (3rd ed., p. 80). Columbus, OH: Merrill.

Lindquist, M. M. (1987). Strategic teaching in mathematics. In B. F. Jones, A. S. Palincsar, D. S. Ogle, & E. G. Carr (Eds.), *Strategic Teaching and Learning* (pp. 111–134). Alexandria, VA: Association for Supervision and Curriculum Development.

Long, N. J. (1994). Inclusion: Formula for failure? *The Journal of Emotional and Behavioral Problems, 3*(3), 19–23.

Lovitt. T. (1991). *Preventing school dropouts: Tactics for at-risk, remedial, and mildly handicapped adolescents.* Austin, TX: PRO-ED.

Mackay, H. (1994). *Why don't people listen?* Sydney, Australia: Pan MacMillan.

Manning, M., & Haddock, P. A. (1988, November). Managing difficult people. *SKY Magazine,* p. 128, 132–134.

Meltzer, L., Roditi, B., Haynes, D. P., Bidle, K. R., Paster, M., & Taber, S. (1996). *Strategies for success: Classroom teaching techniques for students with learning problems.* Austin, TX: PRO-ED.

Nevin, A., Thousand, J., Paolucci-Whitcomb, P., & Villa, R. (1990). Collaborative consultation: Empowering public school personnel to provide hetereogenous schooling for all—or, Who rang that bell? *Journal of Educational and Psychological Consultation, 1*(1), 41–67.

Palincsar, A. S., & Brown, A. L. (1984). Reciprocal teaching of comprehension-fostering and comprehension-monitoring activities. *Cognition and Instruction, 1*(2), 117–175.

Pokras, S. (1989). *Systematic problem-solving and decision-making.* Los Altos, CA: Crisp.

Provus, M. (1971). *The discrepancy evaluation model.* Berkeley, CA: McCutchan.

Putnam, J. W., Spiegel, A. N., & Bruininks, R. H. (1995). Future directions in education and inclusion of students with disabilities: A Delphi investigation. *Exceptional Children, 61*(6), 553–576.

Resnick, L. (1987). *Education and learning to think. 1987 ASCD Yearbook.* Alexandria, VA: Association for Supervision and Curriculum Development.

Roy, P., & O'Brien, P. (1989, November). *Collaborative school: What! So what! Now what!* Paper presented at the annual conference of the National Staff Development Council, Anaheim, CA.

Sage, D. (Ed). (1993). It means more than mainstreaming . . . *Inclusion Times, 1*(1), 2.

Saver, K., & Downes, B. (1990). Pit Crew: A model for teacher collaboration in an elementary school. *The Consulting Edge, 2*(2), 1–3.

Schloss, P. J. (1992). Mainstreaming revisited. *The Elementary School Journal, 92*(3), 233–244.

Sharan, S. (1980). Cooperative learning in small groups: Recent methods and effects on achievement, attitudes, and ethnic relations. *Review of Educational Research, 50*(2), 241–271.

Slavin, R. E. (1981). Synthesis of research on cooperative learning. *Educational Leadership, 38,* 655–660.

Slavin, R. E. (1984). Review of cooperative learning research. *Review of Educational Research, 50*(2), 315–342.

Slavin, R. E., Madden, N. A., & Stevens, R. J. (1990). Cooperative learning models for the 3 R's. *Educational Leadership, 47*(4), 22–28.

Smith, S. C., & Scott, J. L. (1990). The *collaborative school.* Eugene: University of Oregon, ERIC Clearinghouse on Educational Management.

Thousand, J., & Villa, R. (1990). Sharing expertise and responsibilities through teaching teams. In W. Stainback & S. Stainback (Eds.), *Network supports for inclusive schooling: Interdependent integrated education* (pp. 151–166). Baltimore: Brookes.

Thousand, J., Villa, R., & Nevin, A. (1994). *Creativity and collaborative learning: A practical guide to empowering students and teachers.* Baltimore: Brookes.

Vaughn, S., & Schumm, J. S. (1995). Responsible inclusion for students with learning disabilities. *Journal of Learning Disabilities, 28*(5), 264–270.

Welch, M., Richards, G., Okada, T., Richards, J., & Prescott, S. (1995). A consultation and paraprofessional pull-in system of service delivery: A report on student outcomes and teacher satisfaction. *Remedial and Special Education, 16,* 15–28.

West, J. F., & Cannon, G. (1988). Essential collaborative consultation competencies for regular and special educators. *Journal of Learning Disabilities, 21*(1), 56–63, 28.

West, J. F., & Idol, L. (1990). Collaborative consultation in the education of mildly handicapped and at-risk students. *Remedial and Special Education, 11*(1), 22–31.

West, J. F., Idol, L., & Cannon, G. (1989). *Collaboration in the schools: An inservice and preservice curriculum for teachers, support staff, and administrators.* Austin, TX: PRO-ED.

Wiederholt, J. L., & Chamberlain, S. P. (1989). A critical analysis of resource programs. *Remedial and Special Education, 10*(6), 15–37.

INDEX

ABOUT THE AUTHOR

◆ **Dr. Lorna Idol** is a speaker, consultant, and author in the areas of creating collaborative and inclusive schools, collaborative consultation, effective instruction of difficult-to teach students, and reading/learning disabilities. She has been an associate professor at the University of Illinois at Champaign-Urbana, a special education teacher, and is currently an adjunct professor at The University of Texas at Austin. She has written extensively in education journals and books in the area of collaborative consultation, as well as on effective instruction, remedial reading, and learning disabilities.

The Collaborative Consultation model has been implemented in numerous schools in the United States, Canada, and Australia. Dr. Idol developed the Resource/Consulting Teacher model while a professor at the University of Illinois. Dr. Idol serves as consultant to numerous school agencies, state departments of education, university teacher preparation programs, and corporate professional development programs.

Other Books and Materials by Lorna Idol and Co-authors

Idol, L., Nevin A., & Paolucci-Whitcomb, P. (2000). *Collaborative consultation* (3rd ed.). Austin, TX: PRO-ED.

Idol, L., Nevin A., & Paolucci-Whitcomb, P. (1999). *Models of curriculum-based assessment* (3rd ed.). Austin, TX: PRO-ED.

Idol, L. (1997). *Reading Success: A specialized literacy program for students with challenging reading needs*. Austin, TX: PRO-ED.

Idol, L. (1993). *Special educator's consultation handbook* (2nd ed.). Austin, TX: PRO-ED.

Idol, L., & West, J. F. (1993). *Effective instruction of difficult-to-teach students: An inservice and preservice professional development program for classroom, remedial, and special education teachers*. Austin, TX: PRO-ED.

Idol, L., & Jones, B. F. (Eds.). (1991). *Educational values and cognitive instruction: Implications for reform*. Hillsdale, NJ: Erlbaum.

Jones, B. F., & Idol, L. (Eds.). (1990). *Dimensions of thinking and cognitive instruction*. Hillsdale, NJ: Erlbaum.

Idol, L., & West, J. F. (1989). *Collaboration in the schools consultation: The problem-solving process* [Video] Austin, TX: PRO-ED.

West, J. F., Idol, L., & Cannon, G. (1989). *Collaboration in the schools: Communicating, interacting, and problem solving*. Austin, TX: PRO-ED.

Idol, L. (Ed.)(1987). *Grace Fernald's remedial techniques in basic school subjects*. Austin, TX: PRO-ED.